Staying Sane™

When Your FAMILY COMES TO VISIT

ALSO IN THE STAYING SANE™ SERIES

Staying Sane When You're Dieting

Staying Sane When You're Quitting Smoking

Staying Sane™ When Your FAMILY COMES TO VISIT

Pamela K. Brodowsky
Evelyn M. Fazio

A Member of the Perseus Books Group

Set in 12-point New Baskerville by the Perseus Books Group

Library of Congress Cataloging-in-Publication Data

Brodowsky, Pamela K.
Staying sane when your family comes to visit / Pamela K. Brodowsky, Evelyn M. Fazio.—1st Da Capo Press ed.
p. cm. — (Staying sane)
ISBN-13: 978-0-7382-1036-0 (isbn-13; pbk. : alk. paper)
ISBN-10: 0-7382-1036-6 (isbn-10; pbk. : alk. paper) 1. Family–Psychological aspects. 2. Adult children–Family relationships. 3. Intergenerational relations. 4. Interpersonal relations. 5. Holiday stress. 6. Stress (Psychology) I. Fazio, Evelyn M. II. Title.
HQ734.B8384 2005
306.87—dc22
2005020416

First Da Capo Press edition 2005

Published by Da Capo Press
A Member of the Perseus Books Group
www.dacapopress.com

Da Capo Press books are available at special discounts for bulk purchases in the U.S. by corporations, institutions, and other organizations. For more information, please contact the Special Markets Department at the Perseus Books Group, 11 Cambridge Center, Cambridge, MA 02142, or call (800) 255-1514 or (617) 252-5298, or e-mail special.markets@perseusbooks.com.

1 2 3 4 5 6 7 8 9—08 07 06 05

To follow your dream is to live your dream.

My first of many thanks goes to my father. Though he is no longer among us, I truly feel that without his inspiration and the memories of my time spent with him I would have never made it to living my dreams; to you, my undying gratitude. My next thank you goes to my husband, Edward, for the many long conversations, for hashing and rehashing with me the wealth of ideas that flow through the creative side of my brain. For keeping your comments to yourself when I am spending more time with my keyboard than with you. For always being by my side, and for seeing all my dreams as I see them myself, my undying love goes to you. To my children, Sarah and Jake, you are truly the loves of my life and I am so very proud of both of you. And last, but certainly not least, Evelyn, my partner, friend, and other half, for being game for just about anything and so like myself that it's scary. My hat goes off to you, Cheech.

—PAM

This book is dedicated to my parents, the best anyone could have. Although my father no longer walks the Earth, he's always here in my heart. Thanks for always being there with love, advice, and support when I needed it, and especially for always making me laugh! And Pam, this book is dedicated to you, too. Only you could have talked me into this and made it a lot of fun, too. My cowboy hat is off to you, too!

—EVELYN

Contents

About the Staying Sane Series

The Staying Sane series is a collection of funny, irreverent, light-hearted, yet sassy, advice-laden books that are dedicated to finding the silver lining in the annoying, frustrating, or trying situations we all encounter every day.

The Staying Sane series shows you how to look for—and find—the humor and enlightenment in nearly every situation—you need only be open to seeing it. Let's face it: We all experience difficult or trying times in our lives, and that's precisely why we've developed the Staying Sane series.

We want you to know that we've been through all kinds of demented things ourselves (oh, have we ever!), and we and our contributors plan to focus each volume on a specific topic to help you cope with some of the most trying, most typical—and most common—situations we all face at one point or another as we try to get through life.

The Staying Sane series' intention, unlike other books, is to shed light on difficult situations, to bring laughter to people who are caught in a web of frustration and petty annoyances, and to provide help, advice, and answers for every situation. At the same time, we want to let readers know that they are not the only ones who've suffered through these irritating episodes or situations. As laughter is truly the best medicine, the Staying Sane series will help you get through whatever comes up with as few dents and bruises as possible, and with your family relationships and friendships still intact.

Just hearing about other people's problems usually makes our own seem trivial by comparison, making us realize that things aren't really so bad. What's more, by reading about the scores of other people who've had the same or worse experience, we are able to get a more realistic perspective and regain our sense of proportion—all because we've been able to step back and see that things really could be much worse. And besides, misery loves company, doesn't it?

Staying sane it isn't as hard as you think. Keeping it together when all hell breaks loose is just part of life—something we have to do every day if we're living on planet Earth.

But one thing to keep in mind is that there is always someone else out there who is also on the edge of loosing it. Our lives are complicated, but this doesn't mean we can't laugh at our problems—it can really help make them seem smaller and less overwhelming.

So when things really are getting out of hand and you just don't think you can take it anymore, pick up a copy of one of the Staying Sane titles. It may be just what you need to keep from going off the deep end. We'll be right there with you, helping you cope!

Let Us Know

We would be delighted to hear from you about your reactions to the stories in this and all the other Staying Sane books. Please let us know which stories you liked the most and how they related to your life.

Please send us your stories for upcoming volumes of the Staying Sane series. Is there a topic you'd like us to cover? If so, let us know what you're looking for. We'll do our best to get a book into the works for you. We can be reached directly by email at:

submission@staying-sane.com

You can also visit us on the Web at:

www.staying-sane.com

We look forward to hearing from you!

Pam and Evelyn

About *Staying Sane When Your Family Comes to Visit*

Nothing is more wonderful than having fun with your family. You have all known each other forever, and you are so comfortable together that there's none of the awkward, getting-to-know-you formality or stiffness. But this also means that family members can really drive you crazy simply because they know how—after all, they've had years of practice!

What exactly is it about family and friends that can sometimes drive you crazy? Is it because some of them just show up at any time, unannounced, for a long and inconvenient visit—just when you're trying to finish that complicated project that you've been working on for weeks? Or is it because they think it's no problem when they want to crash at your place and be waited on, whenever they want, regardless of your desperate need to finish your taxes and it's 10:00 p.m. on April 14?

Why don't they realize that they're pushing you to the limit of what's left of your sanity by invading your space, eating what's left of the food in your fridge, finishing off that last bottle of your best wine, or giving you unwanted advice when you would rather eat glass or sleep on a bed of nails than listen to the same old nonsense for the 274th time?

Although we can't answer those questions for *your* family, we can tell you that it's happened to us, too, and plenty of times. We can also guarantee that we can get you laughing about it—or something like it—if you read the hilarious stories in *Staying Sane When Your Family Comes to Visit.*

When your in-laws, cousins, or siblings think they are authorities on just about every subject, we have a way to put it all in the proper, hilarious perspective. If you have singles giving you marriage advice, people without kids giving you parenting advice, parents telling you how you should live your life, and a sister who hasn't had a date in years giving you dating advice, we understand, sympathize—and help you laugh about it. After all, we've been there, done that.

Whatever it is that these well-meaning folks come up with, we can crack you up with a similar story—and some sassy advice to help you deal with the situation.

All you have to do is look at the table of contents and find the related chapter, sink down into your favorite comfy chair with a cup of coffee or tea (or beer, or wine, or even Thorazine if it's really bad!), and you're all set.

Because that's when *Staying Sane When Your Family Comes to Visit* charges in to rescue you. How? Because all the Staying Sane stories you'll find in this book come directly from people who have walked in your shoes or found themselves in a similar situation. Every one of them endured the exasperating meddling, annoyance, and insanity that you are now facing, and they have all triumphantly survived. Yes, they may be battle-scarred, but they're still here, and they want you to realize that you will be, too; you'll get through just as they did, but you'll have an advantage: You'll have spent some time laughing, which always helps, and you'll have garnered some useful insights and advice from the experts—the survivors who've had hands-on experience with that same pesky problem.

These veterans are ready and eager to share their wisdom and enlightenment. They know what it's like, they know what you're going through, and they, too, have pulled out their hair (if they had any to begin with). Now you can benefit from all that experience.

Besides, just like your ornery relatives, they love to give advice. It's human nature and we can't help it—

we all like to talk about ourselves. And just think—someday, if you read this book, of course—you may be able to help someone else, just the way these folks helped you! That's the best kind of payback we can think of.

And just in case you're not convinced yet, would you like to see just how much you need this book? Try taking our following Sanity Quiz and see how you do.

SANITY QUIZ

1. Do you often feel like pulling your hair out when your family is coming to dinner?
2. Does the mere idea of a holiday visit to a family member make you develop an eye twitch?
3. Are you having night sweats just thinking about your sibling's upcoming visit because they're bringing the entire flock of kids to stay with you?
4. Has the amount of gray in your hair increased recently because you have to spend the weekend babysitting the nephews who won't eat anything but fishsticks?
5. Is your mother the mother from hell, but only at your house?
6. Do you feel the need to scream when your cousin brings his python to your son's graduation from kindergarten?

7. Does nothing you say or do seem to be heard over the din of the TV because your brother-in-law won't let you have the remote when he moves in for the weekend?
8. Are you going bald trying to deal with those family fights and disputes that all descend on your home?
9. Do you think you've been dealt a bad-relative hand each time you all get together?
10. Do you really think you are the only one who has these problems?

If you answered yes to any of these questions, then *Staying Sane When Your Family Comes to Visit* is the book for you!

Because for whatever reason you're ready to scream, from having unruly relatives camped out on your couch, to those in-laws who insist on bringing their pets, to cousins with impossible brats in tow, to people who won't eat anything with the letter *r* in its name (except on Wednesday!), we have something for you!

If you have friends who won't go home, if you have relatives who stick you on the sofa bed with the metal bars that hit every body part each time you move (you know the one we're talking about!), if you develop hives just by thinking about the prospect of a family holiday gathering, if you have a sister-in-law who won't move her butt once she crosses your threshold because she thinks she's on vacation, or if you can't stop your grandmother from "helping" you make the soup, then we have some stories for you, along with some sensible and expert advice from the survivors. You can take them to heart and come through with flying colors.

So relax and enjoy the ride—you'll feel better in practically no time at all!

1

When Your Family Visits You

Your family is coming to visit! Quick, lock the door, pull the shades. Be very, very quiet.

Maybe they will just go away. Fat chance! Your car's in the driveway—they know you're there. Hunker down: It's going to be a long ride.

To properly gauge your reaction to this unexpected news, take the following quiz:

Sanity Quiz

It's 7:00 p.m. on Saturday night. You have just sat down to take your first bite of dinner when the phone rings. It's your family. They are in the neighborhood and they figured they would drop in for a visit.

Do you

A. lock the doors
B. turn off the lights
C. run out the back door
D. all of the above

Which answer did you pick?

No matter which answer you chose, you need to read the following Staying Sane stories to find out how to cope, what to do, and, most important, how to stay sane when the family does show up. Because they will. In fact, they are on their way right now!

As you laugh your way through these stories, you'll see that often the best way to cope is to expect the unexpected, be prepared for almost anything, be as flexible as possible, and try to enjoy your visitors without gritting your teeth or getting the fur flying! In addition to the laughter of recognition, you'll also find some good practical advice from people who've been there and survived!

Danger: Men Working!

P. J. Dempsey

NEVER UNDERESTIMATE WHAT TWO siblings can cook up—no matter how old they are.

When I was ten years old, my dad's youngest brother came to visit us in Pittsburgh. My Uncle Henry had just begun work as a mechanic and my dad saw this as an opportunity to enlist his help in a money-saving do-it-yourself project; unfortunately, as the project proceeded it escalated into entertainment for the entire neighborhood and nearly ended my parents' marriage.

You see, my dad had decided to save himself from buying a new car by replacing the engine in our 1954 Plymouth. He and my uncle had convinced themselves not only that they would be able to do this but also that the job would be easy; in reality, however, changing a car engine at home is akin to trying to perform an organ transplant with garden tools.

Need I mention that car engines are heavy? And though they might be simple enough to detach and reattach, the trick is getting the new one actually to power the car!

After convincing my mother, who was not an easy sell, that changing a car engine would be a task they could accomplish, my dad and my uncle began work. The first hurdle was to remove the broken engine. Now, garages are equipped with machines capable of lifting heavy objects, such as engines, from a car. The extent of our special weight-bearing machinery was a swing set. Yes, a swing set.

Problem one, the car was on the street and the swing set was in the yard, but this was no problem for the Einstein brothers: They took out a portion of our fence and pushed the car up onto the curb, over the sidewalk, and into our yard so that the hood was under the swing set. Heavy chains, pulleys, and hooks were attached—but the only thing that moved was the metal pipe on top of the swing set: to everyone's horror, it buckled in the middle.

My mother's shrieks announced this circus act to the neighborhood, and from that day on, the guys had an audience.

Now the pipe on the swing set had to be replaced and the car put back on the street. We lived in the city, so there was no driveway or garage in which to work. Our street was cobblestone and narrow, with just enough room for the cars parked on both sides; trolley tracks ran down the middle and the trolley thundered through every twenty minutes.

After the fiasco with the flimsy swing set, the brothers bought heavy wood to build something sturdy enough to lift a car engine, a structure my mother referred to as "the gallows." The construction took considerable time, effort, and—surprise—more money than expected. It held up all traffic—automobile, trolley, and pedestrian—as it extended out on to the sidewalk.

In the end, the old engine was removed and a "new" engine was inserted. It didn't work. More fiddling, but the car refused to move.

I'm not quite sure what happened after that, but one day I came home from school and found that we had another car—a green-and-white 1956 Chevrolet. We didn't talk about the other car ever again.

And after spending an entire summer on this disastrous project, my uncle finally went home. My mother's feathers were ruffled for some time to come, and Dad was in the dog house for weeks afterwards. As for Uncle Henry, well, he didn't come back for a while . . . until the *next* project begged for his "help." But that's another story altogether!

SURVIVAL HINTS

1. Men should not be allowed to hatch money-saving schemes without supervision.
2. Those "Danger—Men Working" signs were made out of necessity—actually they should just say, "Danger—Men Thinking"!
3. Never underestimate the trouble brothers can get into.
4. Remember that an older brother can always force a younger brother to do stupid stuff; men need accomplices.

Loved Ones

Edward F. Fitzgerald

"YES, DEFINITELY THE LARGE size. A gallon? Perfect."

"*George!* Who's that on the phone?"

"Excuse me a minute. *The hardware store, Hon—I'll just be a moment.* Will the label say, 'Rat Poison' right on it? Well, no matter, I can fix that. My real question is will you be able to taste it in soup?"

Now before you jump to any conclusions about this snippet from the tape compiled by the Department of Homeland Security, in fairness now, you have to know what preceded that call.

It had been a long day at the fruit-juice store (I love telling people I pop cherries for a living), and I had just settled down with a large single malt when my wife, Pittypat, also known as "Thc Force," ambled in. She was pretending to dust the bookcase. That should have been a tip—Pittypat cleaning. I would have heard if we were going to use the living room for a wake.

"She's arriving tomorrow," she told me.

"Who?" I asked, the figurative icicle sliding down my neck.

"I *told* you last week," she lied. "You never listen. My sister."

"Echinacea!" I choked, spitting scotch onto my ancient and treasured Perry Como cardigan. *"That* health nut? Oh, my God!"

"It's just for two weeks."

I knew I was doomed, but I tried. "But her husband and the kids will miss her terribly."

An awful pause.

"No, they won't," Pittypat said in a tiny, barely audible voice.

"Oh, no! She's not bringing *them,* too? That sponge, Humpy, her worser half? For *two weeks!*"

"But you *like* Humphrey, George."

"Like him? That twit borrowed money from me daily on the last visit. Used to call me 'ATM.'"

"He was out of work, Dear, a little short."

"Short? He's bloody dwarfish."

"He has a job now."

"What, bell ringer at Notre Dame? Are they really bringing Flobbo and Kaka?"

"*George.* You know it's Rollo and Katya. And you enjoyed Rollo last time. You even played soccer with him."

"That's true. One more good kick and I'd have put him through the goalposts, but old Humpy had to get in the way."

"Katya is a darling six-year-old. You two cooked dinner last time, while I was at the emergency room with Rollo. You enjoyed that."

"I didn't. The little blight wouldn't stay in the pot. Turn my back for a second to get more onions and potatoes and she was out and running."

"What?"

"I said, 'Like as not, in this weather she'll be out and sunning.' Damn. I just remembered. Funny how these things slip the mind. I'm supposed to leave tomorrow for that conference . . . uh, seminar . . . meeting . . . jail term . . . something important."

"*George.*"

"No, really. It's in Cincinnati. No one lies about having to go to Cincinnati. It's only for a month. I'll bring back local gifts. Uh, draft paper with all those little lines. Pencils. A bust of Jerry Springer. *Please!*"

"You know, though," Pittypat mused, ignoring me, "I'm sorry now we turned the second spare room into my sewing and macramé studio. We have no place to put the kids. Well, no problem. It's only for two weeks. Echinacea and Katya and I will take *our* room, and you and Humphrey and Rollo can share the double bed in the guest room—it's really quite spacious if you avoid the dip in the middle. You'll need the rubber sheet for Rollo, of course. George, *please* stop crying. It's *so* unmanly."

Well, now you have the preamble to my telephone call to the poison center, or hardware store as some of you less motivated shoppers prefer to call it.

And so the die is cast, the visit is inevitable, the plague is imminent—what the hell do you do?

Well, luckily, I happen to have right here in my trembling fist some simple suggestions that will see you through. (If not, don't forget the hardware store.)

SURVIVAL HINTS

1. *Stock the Larder.* Find out in advance what they like, and do not like, to eat and drink, so you will be ready to sail through the first two days of meals and snacks. Don't wait until they have arrived or you will find yourself running off to the store at the dinner hour, standing in long lines, and probably getting soaked in rain or snow to boot. During your absence, your spouse will be

sitting nose-to-nose with the relatives recapping the good old days and all the latest gossip while an unwatched and excited bratpack (made up of your children and the visiting kids) will be efficiently dismantling your entire house. They will be discovering that a broken lamp will not flush down the toilet, and the other things they've broken they'll be hiding in bottom drawers. If you are sent out to the store within the first two hours after the arrival of visiting guests, do not stop at the store—just keep going. Cincinnati will look better than what is left of your house when you get back, I promise you.

2. *Make the First Meal Simple.* Avoid elaborate dishes and complicated cooking for the arrival dinner so that you do not set too high a standard for subsequent meals during the visit! Or cook ahead of time so that the food can be eaten cold. If you got lucky and picked up the meat course that day, be sure the "tire treads" don't show when it's on the platter. Stuff the kids' faces all day with potato chips, bologna, and buckets of cheese whiz. They'll all be upstairs puking when you break out the expensive ham and turkey. Never watch relatives eat—that can be just too scary. Keep your head down and pretend to be saying a long grace. When the adults are finally

drunk and the intra-family fights are underway, *simply rise above them*. You can do this with the help of certain powders that I will name for you if you send me five dollars and a SASE. Remember—enjoy yourself no matter what because all good things come to an end.

3. *Provide and Suggest Games.* Don't let long, awful lulls embarrass everyone. Take the kiddies down to the basement and give them plenty to play with—metal-tipped darts, bows and arrows, lots of sharp sticks—then get out and lock the door. Later, with most of the kids at the hospital or in bed in splints, throw a party for the adults and invite your neighbors over to help entertain the in-laws. Now that you are free of the kids and the adults are well-oiled, suggest fun games such as "Guess My Bra Size!" "What Have I Got In My Pants?" and the always popular "Watch Me Strip!" Suggestions like that will cause your wife to say "Isn't he a caution?"—especially if most of the women there are younger and thinner than she is. In my experience, that's when the real fun starts. In addition to the fun of this moment, this is also a sure-fire way to get your unwanted guests to leave early the next day; there's nothing like an emerging hangover to send them packing.

4. *Hide and Seek.* This belongs in a separate category from the above because this game is played only by the hosts—usually on about the third day of the two-week visit. This is when you and your spouse get up real, real early, pack a bag, and very quietly sneak out and drive to the airport. The fun note you leave on the front door says:

   "Joke's on you, guys! We're off to Aruba. Take good care of our kids and help yourself to what's in the fridge, which, as you know, is empty! Ha, ha!"

Well, that pretty well does it, I guess, as long as you remember one important thing—be sure to lie to your visitors about the date and time you will be arriving home. You don't need a nasty scene at the airport with disgruntled relatives just when you want to display your tan and tropical hats and make the regular commuters eat their hearts out.

Oh, by the way, you're probably wondering about the scream—the scream that brought the police and an ambulance to our house the day Pittypat first told me about her sister's pending visit. Did I forget to tell you about that?

It's easy to explain. I was just playing my last ace-in-the-hole, reminding Pittypat about how much trouble houseguests can be. Reminding her that—let's face it—she really *does* hate to cook. That's when Pittypat pulled the pin.

"Now don't you worry your handsome head about things like that, George—*my mother's* coming to help out!"

Ed Fitzgerald is the author of *Bank's Bandits: The Untold Story of The Original Green Berets.*

The In-laws' Post-Honeymoon Visit

Arline Simpson

AS WE WERE ON our way home from our wonderful honeymoon in Acapulco, Mexico, in 1964, a gentleman approached us in the airport at Mexico City and asked whether we were going to New York. "Yes," we answered rather enthusiastically, "Why do you want to know?"

The gentlemen said he had a package that had to be delivered, and if we would be kind enough to take it with us, he would compensate us by treating us to whatever we wanted from the duty free shop. These were simpler times, and nobody worried about terrorism.

My husband asked, "Can I get some extra liquor to take back?" The gentlemen said, "Yes, of course, you can have what you want."

Then my husband, being an attorney, asked, "What's in the package? Is it legal?"

The gentlemen replied, "It's the master print of the new John Huston film, *Night of the Iguana,* starring Ava Gardner, and there will be a courier waiting at the airport in New York to pick it up."

Rather excitedly, we accepted the big can of film and, accompanied by the gentleman, went to the duty free shop, where we purchased our extra bottles of liquor.

We arrived home from Mexico at approximately 3:00 a.m. on a Sunday morning, dropped our luggage, and went straight to bed.

It seemed we were asleep for only an hour when the doorbell rang. I jumped up and ran to answer it.

It was my in-laws and their neighbors.

Shocked, I asked, "What are you doing here at this hour?" And then, "What time is it anyway?"

My father-in-law replied, "It's seven-thirty. We thought you would be up."

I sighed deeply and called my husband, who staggered into the hall in a daze.

"Mom, Dad, what's wrong?" he asked.

"Nothing, Son," said my father-in-law. "We just wanted to welcome you home."

After a few minutes of trying to focus my eyes, I gathered my wits, welcomed them and their neighbors to our new home, and offered them coffee.

While the coffee was brewing, my mother-in-law started opening my cabinets and showing her neighbors my dishes, explaining, "Oh, my sister-in-law gave them these dishes, and see these towels, they're from our cousin in Israel."

She showed her neighbors every room in our apartment, and told them who gave us what.

I was stunned and speechless—and so was my husband. On top of it all, we were dying to tell them about transporting the latest Ava Gardner film back to New York, but never had the chance because they were too busy running around the apartment opening closets and drawers and showing off our gifts from their relatives and friends!

After about an hour and a half of this insanity, they all finally, blessedly, left.

I looked at my husband in total disbelief over what had just happened and said, "What the hell was that all about?"

He said, "I don't know, but they're gone, I'm tired, and I'm going back to sleep."

I thought this peculiar behavior was completely out of character for my in-laws, but soon found out that it wasn't. Eventually, I realized that they had acted out of pride rather than nosiness that morning, and had meant no harm or inconvenience. We had always had a wonderful relationship, and it flourished for the rest of their lives.

As for *Night of the Iguana,* it was nominated for four Academy Awards, and it actually won an Oscar. We were pleased, in some small way, to have helped it find its place in Hollywood history!

I also learned that, no matter what happens, the best thing to do when unexpected guests arrive is to offer a kiss hello and make some coffee.

SURVIVAL HINTS

1. With in-laws, expect the unexpected.
2. If the surprising behavior or event isn't offensive, just be patient until it's over.
3. Always be as flexible as possible.
4. Try not to let anything throw you off balance, unless it's hurtful or mean.
5. Don't forget to be hospitable—get that coffee going. The sooner you serve it, the sooner they'll go home!

Aunt Zina's Sunday Best

Evelyn M. Fazio

WHEN I WAS GROWING UP, we had lots of company, and many visitors who were family or almost family. One of the most frequent visitors was my godmother, known as Aunt Zina. She was a cousin on my mother's side, but because she was my godmother, she was given the title of aunt.

Aunt Zina was a widow. A big widow—very big. She weighed in at more than two hundred pounds, by all estimates, and she was only about five feet tall at best. She was rotund, to say the least.

Being a widow of the Italian variety, Aunt Zina wore black from head to toe. Well, I shouldn't say head. Her hair was bright orange. Not carrot orange—that's nowhere near as bright as I mean—it was more like your-dinner's-in-flames-on-top-of-the-stove orange! You could almost feel the heat radiating off it, and forget about the sun glare if you were outside.

Aunt Zina lived in the next town but liked to visit my parents every Sunday, no matter what, just as she did when Uncle Jack was alive. She'd call, and then she'd have her daughter drop her off so that she could spend the afternoon with us. And for the duration of these lengthy layovers, she'd tell stories about her sisters and their kids—sometimes in excruciating detail.

Now, at the time, we had a big dog, Duke, who was a wonderful, lovable, slobbering, tear-flinging, shedding, gas-passing giant. Naturally, he was included in everything: family vacations at the beach, car trips, family meals, and meals at which we entertained guests. Duke had the run of the house, and was the maitre d' of the establishment. He greeted all guests, decided who got past the door, and then sat at (or on) the feet of his favorites. He also had his choice of furniture to sleep on, sleep being his occupation for about 75 percent of the time.

On the Sunday in question, Aunt Zina showed up a little earlier than usual, and Mom hadn't finished her touchup with the vacuum cleaner. Meanwhile, Duke had carefully deposited his nightly quota of fawn-colored stiff hair onto his favorite chair. I'll never know why they didn't put a throw or some kind of cover over that chair, but I digress.

Aunt Zina appeared at the door. Naturally, Duke jumped up from his chair and went into his "meet and greet" routine, with much barking, wiggling, snorting, dancing, and the other ecstatic displays to which he was inclined.

We should all have seen what was coming next: Aunt Zina headed straight for Duke's chair and sat down. Duke didn't seem to mind; he just took his bone and plopped into the middle of the living-room floor, Sphinx-like, to eat his snack.

Aunt Zina remained regally enthroned in the Hair Chair for several hours, telling stories as usual, and got up again only when her ride home at last appeared. As she walked down the front steps to the sidewalk, my parents exchanged a look of horror: She was now wearing a black-fronted, reddish-brown-backed dress—custom redesigned à la Duke!

They closed the door and nearly collapsed with laughter. Duke didn't see what was so funny; with a snort, he climbed back up into *his* chair and took a nice long nap.

Aunt Zina never complained, and she was back again the following Sunday, once again in her best black ensemble. I guess she had figured it was worth being covered in dog hair to have her regular Sunday audience, and we did our best to stay awake.

SURVIVAL HINTS

1. If your pets use the furniture, warn your guests so that they can dress and sit accordingly.
2. If your animals shed, try to cover your furniture with throws, blankets, or towels; you can remove them for company.
3. Keep lots of lint rollers around to pick up pet hair that gets on your guests!
4. Invest in a very good vacuum cleaner and use it *before* your guests arrive.

Mother Comes to New York

Lelia Kinsky

I WAS IN MY EARLY twenties, and had come East from California to go to school in New England. After graduation, I settled in New York City, and my mother came to visit. She was always the fussy sort, one who found fault with everything. And she outdid herself on this visit, picking on my furniture, my clothes, my street, neighborhood, and my landlord. She even complained about the weather, as if I could do anything about that!

In spite of her disdain for nearly everything, Mom wanted to see all the sights. She had a long list of items to check off, and insisted that we hit them all, no matter what. Maybe she needed new things to pick on and was bored with me and my tiny walk-up apartment!

I was at the point, early in my career, where I needed more than one job if I was to pay the rent and eat as well. Entertainment consisted of network television (no cable) and books from the library. My life was Spartan, but it was mine.

So that I could spend time with Mother, and despite the disapproval of my ogre of a boss, I managed to take time off from my full-time job, and I gave up the freelance work I normally did each week.

Not only that, but I further wrecked what was left of my budget for the upcoming month by showing her all the sights—and I mean all: Broadway shows, the Statue of Liberty, exhibits at the Metropolitan Museum of Art, rides on the Staten Island Ferry and the Circle Line, a baseball game—the works. We managed to have a decent time, when Mother wasn't complaining about the cost of admission, tickets, food, taxis, and everything else—this even though I paid for everything for both of us!

At last, after an action-packed, almost frantically hectic week, the day arrived for Mother's departure and trip back to the West Coast. As I stood there, broke, exhausted, frustrated, and glad it was all over, Mom kissed me goodbye on her way into the cab. Then with an exasperated and slightly bored shrug, she said: "I simply don't know what I'm going to tell my friends when they ask me what I did in New York!"

The cab door closed just in the nick of time—before I had a chance to lunge for her neck and wring it!

After that visit, I resolved to make a full photographic record of further visits, and to collect evidence of all our activities, including ticket stubs, brochures, receipts from restaurants, and any other "expense report" items that might be necessary in helping Mother's memory along—just in case!

SURVIVAL HINTS

1. If you need to see your parents and one or both are fussy, it might be best to see them on their home turf—to preserve your budget and your sanity!
2. Don't invite the fussy parent back—ever.

The Unmanageable Cousin

Felina Katz

WHEN I WAS FOUR years old, my cousin Katie came to stay with us. Her mom had died a few months before, and my parents wanted to help out her father, Dad's brother, who was left with six kids younger than fifteen. Katie was the baby, only three years old. The plan was that if things worked out, the visit could become a permanent one.

Katie's visit sounded like a good idea at the time. But it turned out to be the visit that nearly did my family in. Don't get me wrong, Katie is now a lovely woman, and we love her dearly. But as a child, well . . . she was small, but she packed a wallop! Perhaps the issue was that Katie's mom had been sick for quite a while before she died. Consequently, she was somewhat, um, unmanageable from having less parental guidance than her siblings.

At first it was fun having company. For about the first two hours, anyway. Until Katie decided that the best thing to do with my toys was to dismantle them. But that's too mild a description. Perhaps "demolish" is a better word. Incinerate. Pulverize. Decapitate. Destroy. You get the picture.

Not only that, but Katie's favorite storage place for the dismembered and disemboweled turned out to be the toilet bowl. As you might imagine, this did not go over well with me, her very meticulous, careful, one-year-older cousin, who treated each toy as a family member. Hostilities broke out. Soon, it was open warfare, and we both emerged from battle scratched and bruised, not to mention pissed off in our pint-sized way.

These aquatic activities of Katie's also had an interesting effect on my parents: My father turned apoplectic when he discovered a floating Barbie head in the bowl, and naturally he imagined that all sorts of other things had already flushed down the pipes—from toy car wheels to the batteries from Mr. Machine, along with the checkers and marbles he managed to rescue mid-flush. It wasn't a pretty sight, and he was about ready to flush Katie next.

Mom's reaction, when she wasn't screaming "Katie, don't do that, honey!" was more biblical: She tended to break out in hives and rashes, not to mention sores and possibly boils. Being four, I wasn't good at diagnosis. But I knew she didn't usually have spots. Every last one of Mom's nerves were frayed to the point of shorting out and causing a fire.

As if demolition weren't enough, we were also dismayed, yet strangely awed, by Katie's excessive activity. She had more energy that a nuclear power plant that had solar energy as a backup, and she never seemed to tire, no matter how late she kept us all up, nor how many times she'd jumped off the kitchen table, bounced on the beds, or run around the house naked. Fleet of foot, she was constantly racing, shrieking, or climbing, and that was just inside the house. She even scaled an occasional drape, which doesn't even begin to hint at her athletic prowess. This was a kid who belonged in the Junior Olympics.

Once outside the house, Katie was a really scary force of nature, and one not to be reckoned with if it could be avoided. You never knew where she was going or what she was doing, what she'd leap into, out of, or from under. She needed a lot of supervision. It quickly became a full-time job for all of us to keep her from a horrible fate. Katie's parents had kept a close eye on her, and even they used to leash her to a lamp post in the yard, in direct view of my aunt's kitchen window, when they let her go outside alone. We quickly came to understand why.

Word got out in the neighborhood about the new kid on the block. The other kids suddenly disappeared. Because it was summer, normally playtime was all day, until well after dark. But now, not only did I suddenly have no more friends in what was normally a teeming 1950s baby-boom block, but my only remaining friend was my nemesis, the imp who drove me crazy—Katie.

My father was developing an eye twitch, and my mother's legs were covered with red dots. The doctor said it was nerves. Katie-induced, naturally. Things were getting more edgy every day, and we all held our collective breath, just waiting for the next episode of the Katie Follies to unfold.

The last straw was the day that our neighbor, Mrs. Diana, who lived across the street from our house and was like another grandmother to me, telephoned Mom and told her to come outside—immediately! "Why?" Mom asked. "Because Katie is dangling her legs in the sewer, and if you don't get out here fast, she's going to slide right down and wash away!" Good thing that neighbor was always looking out the window or Katie might have ended up as fish food in the local river!

After dinner that evening, Katie's bag was packed and ready to go, and my uncle came to pick her up and take her home to the rest of the brood, who no doubt missed her very much and were used to her antics. We were happy to see them joyfully reunited, and even happier to see the tail-lights of my uncle's car fade away into the sunset. It had been three months, and we were all glad that the visit had ended.

By nightfall, the block once again resounded with the happy shrieks and laughter of our eleven neighboring kids, who had magically reappeared on the street, and peace had returned to my house.

Before bed, what was left of my decimated toy collection was once again lined up in size order, all the stuffed animals were once again arranged around my pillow, and I returned to my peaceful life once again.

Meanwhile, my father carefully inspected all the plumbing one last time for any remaining evidence of sabotage, checked all the faucets and outlets for booby traps, and then collapsed into his reclining chair to watch the news, a satisfied grin on his face.

Our dog curled up at his feet and even he breathed a sigh of relief. Mom dabbed medication on her sores; I'm happy to report that they were almost totally gone by the end of the month.

SURVIVAL HINTS

1. If you have young relatives coming to visit, have a trial run of a full-day or overnight visit before committing to a long-term stay.
2. Put valuables and any other important objects away and out of harm's reach.
3. Keep your pets under supervision so that a wild child does not hurt them.
4. Be sure your own kids can handle the visit and the disruption.
5. Keep a close watch on your visitor until you know exactly who (or what) you've got on your hands.

Guest-Room Blues

Ted Weaver

WHAT A LOUSY HOST! Our bed was too narrow, the room too small, the bed and door squeaked, and the room had wall-to-wall "stuff," and the television did not work. Was this a bedroom or a junk room?

Maybe a hot shower would help! Water faucets reversed, shower curtain fell on the floor, and then the real bonus: The only towels were the monogrammed display wedding gifts with dust in the folds.

Perhaps the real highlight was the "rock and roll" commode. The seat was so loose I looked for a seatbelt. Then off to bed with the traffic noise just outside the room.

Boy, did we miss our own bed—king-sized, no squeaks—a large room, a bathtub, a shower that worked, clean towels, and a comfortable commode. Yes, we missed all that, as well as the quiet off-street location of our bedroom. But we would have to stay in this place one more night.

We had given our bedroom to two very special friends, to honor them. They would have our best and we would use the guest room.

Many friends and family members had used our guest facilities through the years. We now recalled their haggard morning faces, the unused towels, and we remembered that most kept their suitcases in the car. During the day, they took naps on our couch, and asked to use the half-bath facilities at the other end of the house. They seldom came back.

So far, we have fixed the squeaks, removed the "stuff," installed a seatbelt on the commode, fixed the tub and shower curtain. Still to come (soon) is a king-sized bed, and then we'll properly secure the commode. That leaves only the towels. They have hung there so long that they are faded on one side. They will be replaced by clean new towels and a note added to go ahead and use them.

Road noise? What do you expect? Perfection?

SURVIVAL HINTS

1. If you're planning to offer guests sleeping quarters in your home, be sure to try out the accommodations first just to be sure.
2. Always provide clean, freshly laundered bed linens and towels.
3. Be certain that the plumbing works properly.
4. Make sure your bathroom fixtures are properly attached to the floor!
5. Never, ever, leave clutter, toys, excess clothing, or other suffocating objects in the guest room.
6. Leave drawer and closet space for your guests.

The Tyranny of the Polite

Skip Murphy

WHEN MY POLITE, unobtrusive family asked whether they could come for a visit over the Fourth of July holidays, I thought I knew what to expect. Although I grew up the only child of my father's first marriage and I inherited from my mother a chattiness gene that my half-siblings seem to lack, we're all still fairly similar. Most of us in my immediate family tend toward soft speech and quiet behavior. We don't make loud demands. We don't push our opinions on others. We don't do most of the annoying things that people do on those too-close-for-comfort family sitcoms.

We'd seen a lot of television. We knew the script.

Yet what hadn't been in the script, as far as I could recall, was how damn late we got started the day they arrived. In our script, I, in my capacity as the part-expectant holiday host, spent the better part of my day fielding calls from my friends and trying to make plans with no real idea about when my family was supposed to arrive.

In this story, my family just went missing for forty-eight hours. Their cell phones were out of range, and apparently they'd forgotten about the throwback technology of the pay phone, so I just waited, hour after hour, hoping they'd roll in before sunset. In their minds, no doubt, they thought they were being easy-going, that they weren't "troubling" me with updates from the road. But my own politeness was tethering me to the house in case they arrived suddenly or needed me to meet them somewhere. It was a clash of the considerate.

Eventually, they did arrive, and my self-imposed stress dissolved. My friends had helped me with our plans for the Fourth, and we'd chosen the prime spot in Boulder from which to watch the fireworks: the hills above Chautauqua, where people sat in the shadow of the massive rock formations of the Flatirons and waited for the sun to disappear behind the mountains. It being the prime spot in town, many others had the idea as well, and we had to park several blocks away from the site on the steeply angled streets of the adjoining neighborhood. It was a ten-minute walk at the most, but it was a beautiful, clear evening. I hoped no one would mind.

As we walked, my sister fell into pace with me to let me know that someone *did* mind. "Dad's knees are bothering him," she confided in a whisper.

"What?"

"His knees. And his feet have been hurting him. I don't think he should be doing a lot of walking."

This was the first I'd heard of it. My father was only in his fifties, and in fairly good shape. I never expected that walking a few blocks, even hilly blocks, would be a problem for him. Now I began to wonder just what the three of them had expected to find in Colorado. Once off the eastern plains, it gets hard to sidestep the challenging terrain. We'd only just scratched the surface.

I looked back at Dad, who looked fine to me, though he was a little slow. "Maybe he should cut down on the cigarettes for a few days," I suggested. The thinner air certainly hadn't curbed his habit of smoking at most every opportunity. "I thought we could maybe go for a hike tomorrow. I guess that's out."

She shook her head. "Yeah, I don't think he'd make a hike."

Or most any other popular activity in the state, I thought. *We've just eliminated one of the least strenuous ones.* "I guess we'll just have to think of other things to do," I said.

That's when I began to understand that our pleasant family dynamic might be a problem. It just might prevent my figuring out what my visitors wanted to do during their vacation. My father apparently wouldn't do his own complaining, leaving that as usual to my forbearing sister. Meanwhile, if she was going to be watching out for him, I'd probably never have a good idea of what she wanted to do. And my brother, I knew, was the most hopeless of them all. Out of all of us, he has always been the quietest. I recalled the maddening guessing games our grandparents used to play to find out what he wanted to eat. All they could get from him were shrugs as they offered up one suggestion after another. Every idea was met with blank indifference. I saw similar exchanges for myself in the near future.

In spite of the smoking and the complaining by proxy, however, that evening we made it up the hill, and we had a great time watching the colorful explosions an hour or so later. My friends Elisabeth and Christa had joined us, and the distraction of their company prevented me from wondering whether my soft-spoken trio of relations were enjoying themselves. For the time being, everyone appeared satisfied, although summertime wildfire precautions meant that Dad had to hold off from smoking for a while.

The next day, we were back to facing the challenges of desires and decisions. With the usual Colorado distractions restricted by Dad's still-unexpressed discomfort, I turned to my family for help in planning *their* vacation. "So, do you guys have any ideas about what you want to do? Whatever you want. Just say it."

They looked at each other. They looked at me. They shrugged, thankfully not in unison.

"I don't know," my brother said. "What's there to do here?"

I didn't know what to say. Few places are so identified with their landscape as Colorado. Colorado is mountains. Mountains are what there is to do. Mountain hiking. Mountain climbing. Mountain biking. Skiing in the mountains. Snowshoeing in the mountains. Rafting or kayaking or fishing in the rivers and streams in the mountains. Almost anything anyone had ever wanted to do in the three years I'd been in the state had involved mountains. Some things, such as rafting trips, needed advance preparation that we obviously hadn't done. And almost everything, from what I'd learned, would be difficult for my father to enjoy. For all the options open to us, we might as well have been back in Texas.

There were things to do, but most still involved a lot of walking. Because that's what one does in smallish places with beautiful weather and a lot of scenery.

Because of my father's secret foot affliction, we interspersed walks in tourist-oriented outdoor malls with bouts of sitting and talking. Or the potential for talking. Because that's when the curse of the Murphy family polite silence started to plague me. With our catching up out of the way, they said little except for the occasional random, mundane comment. My responses weren't much better.

"Those mountains look really close."

"Yes, they do."

"I didn't know ya'll had Banana Republics here."

"It's a national chain."

"What's that guy selling?"

"Either incense burners or hash pipes. I never can tell."

Yes, I was bored, but worse, I had the impression that my family was bored. They'd come all this way to visit me and enjoy what my adopted state had to offer. I wanted them to have fun and to see something they couldn't see elsewhere, something other than beautifully landscaped pedestrian malls.

"How about we head up to the mountains?" I asked. My sister looked concerned. My brother shrugged. Dad lit a cigarette.

"We could go up to Estes Park," I continued. "We can drive through the national park. That way, you all can get to see the mountains. You really should."

And so we did. Like many Texas families, mine relies on the pickup truck as a standard means of transport.

Besides my own, we had two others at our disposal because Dad and my sister had driven together and my brother had met them along the way. This meant that whenever the four of us drove somewhere, we had to take at least two vehicles. I led them up the winding roads, through the tiny towns, and on to the entrance of the immense national park. There my brother and I climbed into the bed of Dad's larger truck, and we zipped up the road, where we soon found ourselves jammed behind miles of cars filled with holiday travelers trying without success to get away from the crowds and crush of their daily commutes.

We fell into line. We inched up the mountain road. We tried to be excited by the glorious landscape spilling out all around us. No one admitted to feeling restless and bored. After all, we were in one of the most glorious spots on Earth.

And for a while, the distraction suited us just fine. True, we were polluting the atmosphere when we should have been getting in touch with nature. But given the scenery, we chose to overlook that. After several halting miles, however, the truck's drive train began to slip, making for a jerky ride that the bare metal of the truck bed communicated directly to the backsides of those of us riding in it. The steep grade of the road had begun to take its toll on our flatland vehicle, and Dad declared that we'd come as far as it was safe to go. We'd reached our highest elevation. It was time to turn back.

To make the best of our situation, we made occasional stops during our slow return trip. It gave us at least the illusion of taking in the scenery. I hoped the others were enjoying themselves, but a trek like this one seemed disappointing compared to the outings I'd enjoyed: day-long hikes to distant peaks, jarring mountain bike rides down boulder-strewn paths, daunting descents down freshly dusted ski trails. In light of those experiences, an afternoon on a traffic-clogged mountain road scored only slightly higher than an early-morning mosey to the mailbox.

By the time we got back to where we'd left the second truck, I was in need of some time away from the rest of them. They still showed no more than a vague interest in most of what they saw, and if I couldn't prod them into enthusiasm, I could at least find some relief from the pressures of their passivity. I invented an errand that needed my attention back in Boulder and oriented them toward the longer, scenic route down the mountain. As I drove away, whatever guilt I had at abandoning them dissolved once I realized that I now felt unburdened for the first time since my family's arrival. I rolled down the windows, turned up the stereo, and took every hairpin curve in the road about ten to twenty miles faster than I knew was safe. I didn't care because my reticent relatives would be busy for at least a couple of hours.

Still, my relief was fleeting. Our visit wasn't over. But a thought occurred to me on my solo drive: What I needed was something to place between me and my family. Or some*one.* An outsider. On the first day of the visit, my friends had provided a distraction for us all. I just needed to throw another one of my friends at them. That would keep them busy for a while.

I called Lisa. She already knew that my family was in town and that I wanted her to meet them. When I'd suggested it a couple of days earlier, she said she might have some time for a visit. Now the situation had become dire, and I needed her as a conversational surrogate.

"Seriously," I said, "I need you to come down and meet us. I've run out of things to say to them." I tried to keep the desperate edge out of my voice.

"Well, I guess I might have some time later this afternoon," she said helpfully.

"That would be fantastic," I enthused. "Absolutely any time you have. Really. Please just come meet us when they get back. Please."

"Um . . . okay."

A couple of hours later, I'd rejoined the family and oriented them toward a café with outdoor seating. As I sensed that my questions about their trip back to town would soon run out, I saw Lisa come around the corner toward us. I greeted her as if she were salvation itself and happily introduced her to my clan. And then . . . it was working! She engaged them in conversation. I felt awed that she could command their attention with mere words. The things she knew intuitively to ask were beyond my grasp. She hit them with the hard questions.

"So how are you all enjoying your trip to Colorado?" she asked.

My God, I thought, *I don't know why I never thought of that.* Over the course of my time with the family, I'd somehow lost all sense of normal interactions. Now I was being reminded of how it's done. She asked, they answered. Even better, they started asking *her* questions back! They'd finally come to life again. I sat back to enjoy my coffee, relieved at last of conversational responsibility, and I found myself enjoying my time with my family for the first time that day.

Still, I had one final day to fill with family activity before they headed back home and left me to my life. When we returned to my apartment that evening, I started culling the paper for news of distracting events. I'd given up asking them to help plan their own entertainment. I was just as invested as they were, and it was up to me to save us all.

I came across an announcement about the annual arts festival taking place in the Cherry Creek area of Denver. At last, here was something that didn't challenge the weakened limbs of one's elders and that promised more than a few squirrels' diversion. I made the suggestion almost like a demand. I didn't know how I'd react to objections. Luckily, I got none.

We drove our two-truck caravan down to Denver, found parking, and made our way to the festival. A grid of streets closed off to traffic were strewn with dozens of booths featuring fine arts and upscale concessions. The four of us surveyed the area and, out of family habit, appointed a time and place to meet should we become separated.

In less than a minute, we separated ourselves. Everyone went in a different direction.

I was elated but stunned. I was happy with what had happened, but it gave me pause. There was nothing accidental about our splitting up. Everyone, it seemed, was ready to get off by him or herself for a spell. We were, every one of us, desperate to get away from the others.

And that's when I learned the true meaning of family . . . at least my family. Love them, tolerate them, or contemplate killing them on a back road and blaming it on a crazed drifter, but whatever you're thinking about them, they're probably thinking the same thing about you.

At the end of two hours, we met at the designated spot. I felt a lot better for having had the time and space for myself, and everyone else seemed relieved, too. We were much easier with one another, chatty even by our own standards. I realized then that with just a little effort, I might get through this very special time without telling them that they must never again come within a hundred yards of me. After all, the joys of Christmas were only an uncomfortable six months away.

SURVIVAL HINTS

1. Do the things you want to do when you're hosting family members. It'll keep you engaged and interested.
2. Don't worry about trying to make everyone happy—it's unrealistic.
3. Devise sanity-saving sorties and make a list of possible activities before your guests arrive. Check out the local calendars of shows, fairs, and other seasonal attractions that might interest your visitors.
4. Try to find out what your guests would like to do or be able to do, and also determine ahead of time whether physical limitations will influence the suggested activities you consider.
5. It helps to invite your friends along to make things more interesting, especially if you're surrounded by family visitors. Your friends can provide different viewpoints about the area and serve as conversational surrogates.

2

When You Visit Your Family

Neatness Counts
Ellen Sander

Space Invaders
James Jacobs

Escape Alone and Survive!
Robert Skalpien

Murray's Big Surprise
Irving Schwartz

Humidity Hell
Evelyn M. Fazio

No Frills!
Ginny Chandoha

California-Bound
Anna Jane Grossman

You Can Go Home Again
Flint Wainess

Wedding Party
Ronda Kaysen

It's been scheduled for weeks. You've got to go. But oh, how the dread has set in.

Sanity Quiz

You knew it was coming. Your spouse accepted the invitation months ago. Rather than cause a stir, you just brushed the whole thing off. But how time flies. Today is D-Day and you, you lucky soul, are due to go. You make a last stab at a cheap excuse to get yourself out of this mess.

Do you

A. purposely let all the air out of the tires on your car
B. throw yourself down the stairs in an attempt to break your leg
C. lie to your spouse about the bad case of diarrhea you just came down with
D. all of the above

No matter which answer you picked, you'll find the following funny stories useful in helping you cope with those sometimes dreaded visits to relatives and friends—and to keep your sense of humor. One bit of advice that seems to shine through is be a considerate guest and pay attention to subtle (and not so subtle) hints from your host about what drives them crazy or what makes them happy. Some of these stories are cautionary, but they're all funny and true.

And remember—these writers survived to tell their tales, and at least they can laugh about it now. We hope you will, too.

Neatness Counts

Ellen Sander

I WOULD GUESS THAT most people would like to be able to keep a neat and tidy home. Unfortunately, in this day and age, with how busy we all seem to be, it seems impossible to keep up with clutter.

I am extremely proficient at accumulating clutter. My home is in constant chaos, piled high with all kinds of "stuff." But I was not brought up this way. In fact, my mother was a bit of a neat freak. I would have to say that she was borderline obsessive/compulsive about "a place for everything and everything in its place, or else."

Indeed, my mother did not like to see anything lying around. All objects had to be in a cabinet or a drawer (except her various tchotchkes, which were lovingly and neatly displayed), and all doors and cabinets had to be closed even though every item inside was also exactly where it belonged—no hidden messes there!

If you left something lying around, the object was put neatly into the nearest drawer or closet, never to be seen again (Mom never remembered where she put things; "put away" was all that mattered).

Her kitchen was always immaculate. Even the dish drain was cleared out and put under the sink when everything was finished for the day. As a girl, if I wanted to bake a cake while my mother was at work, I had to make sure that, when she came home, there were no signs of my baking except the finished cake. The kitchen had to be spotless when my mother went to bed. And if I got out of bed in the morning to go to thc bathroom, I came back to a bed already made (so much for going back to sleep). She *definitely* had a problem.

My brother knew how to torture my mother. We called him "The Midnight Marauder." He tended to wake up hungry in the middle of the night. He would make himself a snack, but he would always leave the dishes in the sink. This would drive my mother crazy, which pleased my brother to no end. I think he felt it was his purpose in life to antagonize my mother in any way possible.

His bedroom was a prime example. He was a born slob. His room always looked as if a tornado had gone through it. Clothes littered the floor, magazines and books were everywhere, and usually dirty plates lay scattered here and there. We all told my mother to close the door and let him live that way. Poor dear, she tried so hard, but I think the longest she lasted without breaking down and cleaning up was three days.

When we were all out of the house, married with families of our own, and my father had passed away, my mother decided to downsize. Taking only the things she absolutely couldn't do without, she retired and moved to Florida. For the next twenty years, my husband, kids, and I took our annual vacation to Florida to visit my mother. Alas, my mother's move seemed to make her fetish worse.

Most people thought we were lucky to have somewhere to stay in Florida, but think again. Try to envision a family of four, two adults and two children, crowded into a two-bedroom condo with a neat freak. It's amazing that my poor mother didn't have a nervous breakdown. Despite our knowing how my mother felt about clutter, four extra people couldn't help but create major clutter in a condo. Our luggage and the things we left lying around were more than she could bear.

All Mom's friends would tell her to just ignore our mess and be thankful for our visits. Well, you remember how well my mother dealt with the concept of ignoring a mess. So every year I would do my best to keep things neat, and my mother would do her best to keep her sanity. It was no treat for either of us. As most grandmothers say: "It's wonderful seeing the kids, but it's great when they go home."

One year, when things were a bit tenser than usual, we decided to play a little prank on my mother. All week long she ranted and raved about our leaving things lying around and not closing closet doors. It was one of her more neurotic periods. So on the day we were leaving (a happy day for all), we left my mother a little surprise.

She was walking us out the door to the elevator when my husband decided he had forgotten something. He went back into the apartment and opened *all* the kitchen cabinets and closet doors, then came back out with a devilish gleam in his eye. We got on the elevator and went out to our car, while mother waited on the catwalk, waving goodbye.

As she went back into her apartment, we stopped the car and rolled down the windows. We soon heard a loud scream and then my mother yelled her favorite threat: "You're all out of my will!"

SURVIVAL HINTS

1. Try to accommodate your host's preferences and idiosyncrasies.
2. Be careful not to make too much of a mess when your are a houseguest.
3. Don't be afraid to inject a little humor into the situation if things become tense.

Space Invaders

James Jacobs

A FEW YEARS BACK, while we were having our dream house built, my wife, Gina, and I were invited to stay with my mother-in-law and Gina's stepfather, Ron.

With a tight construction budget, the lure of a free place to stay was tempting.

We initially resisted my mother-in-law's generous offer because she was the quintessential housewife whose home was cleaner than most hospital operating rooms, and also because my wife and her mother hadn't seen eye-to-eye on anything in years. Even so, Gina's mother persisted with her usual mantra: "You're my daughter and any of my children are always welcome in my home."

We eventually relented and moved in. We thought we'd have to stay only for a month or two.

Well, as usual, the construction went much more slowly than expected, and by the sixth month things were becoming stressful, especially for Ron. With each day that passed, this six-foot-two, well-educated IBM executive increasingly suspended all logic with his complaints.

Each time Ron would levy an unusual complaint or nit-pick, Gina's mother would squelch the dissent with the same refrain: "She's my daughter and any of my children are always welcome in my home. If you don't like it then you can leave." Though her message was clear and in our favor (and repeated in our presence!), her taking our side seemed only to make Ron more illogical.

One night Ron came to us and told us that we were running out of water. I asked whether there were problems with the well, but he wasn't referring just to the house. Supposedly he had heard somewhere that the entire town was running out of water. He explained that it was up to Gina and me to cut down on our showers and laundry and thus save the town's water supply.

The next night came the imaginary dust complaint. My wife and I had been sleeping head-to-head on a sectional couch in a finished room over the garage that was heated only with a pellet-burning stove. Each night at about 2:00 a.m., the stove would run out of pellets. From there to sun-up, only our down comforters protected us from frostbite. We really needed those comforters!

But now Ron confronted us about all the dust we were creating with them. Gina and I looked at each other questioningly.

"Dust! You're making too much dust in here. There's dust in fabric and your blankets are made of fabric and that's making this place a dusty mess," he ranted.

I informed him with a smile that the couch and curtains were made of fabric, too. Maybe *they* were making the dust. He didn't see the humor and just stormed out of the room.

So now I'm thinking to myself, "We're creating too much dust with our blankets but he doesn't want us to wash them. Maybe we should just not use them. But then at 2:00 a.m. when the stove shuts down we'll freeze. But then again, if we wash them, then the whole town might go dry and then we won't have water to shower with. Oh, but we're not supposed to shower anyway. And I can already hear Ron complaining about us stinking up his couch because we're not showering, and if we avoid that by sleeping on the floor, I'm sure he'll twist the laws of physics into explaining that we're somehow causing the hardwood to buckle."

I was beginning to think we would have to invoke the Geneva Convention because even prisoners get better treatment than this.

And so it went. Each day Ron came up with more and more creative ways to scrutinize our every move while searching, probing for a way to speed our exit.

Each time the situation started to heat up, Gina's mom immediately went into her spiel: "I've told you over and over again that she's my daughter and she's always welcome at my house. If you don't like it . . . "

One day Ron, that sly dog, interrupted her.

"I'm thinking that it's time we remodel the kitchen. Of course we'll have to wait until the kids are out of here. It'd be too much of an inconvenience with the extra people living in the house."

My mother-in-law continued, "I'll say it again. She's my dau— what did you say? A new kitchen? That includes all new appliances too?"

Two days later, and with the encouragement of Gina's mother, we moved in with my mother . . . and that's another story.

Though it took a few years to become apparent, there was a happy ending. I'm reminded of it every time I hear my wife and her mother making idle chitchat on the phone. Before our never-ending visit, they would talk only when necessary. Their conversations were short and business-like.

But since the long visit, they've actually become friends. Phone calls and visits are much more frequent, and they happen not for any particular reason other than to enjoy each other's company. They still don't see eye-to-eye on everything, but what two people do?

And Ron, though still rough around the edges, has become a wonderful grandfather to our kids. They love their "Poppy." I still can't see how this stern and unemotional man can be reduced to making silly noises and wrestling on the floor with our four-year-old son at the drop of a dime, but I'm glad he does.

Last week, we rearranged our bedroom. While moving things around, I noticed that a fair amount of dust had accumulated.

I paused momentarily and skeptically glanced over at the down comforter on our bed.

SURVIVAL HINTS

1. Don't overstay your welcome, no matter what your hosts tell you about their unlimited generosity.
2. Try to accommodate your hosts' quirks, and learn which ones are exit cues.
3. Don't waste water, electricity, or food, and restock the fridge often, without being asked.
4. Don't create too much dust if you can help it!

Escape Alone and Survive!

Robert "Scoop" Skalpien

WHEN I MARRIED MY WIFE, I was welcomed into a tight circle of three sisters. These sisters are closer than most because their parents were deaf. Heaped on top of that, their father died when the eldest sister was twelve. Their mother had a difficult time dealing with this, so she kind of withdrew. This left the sisters to fend for themselves, and it greatly increased their interconnectivity.

Now whenever we spend time together, which is often, we like to say that we "invade" the other's houses. The luggage that comes with us, the time involved, and the massive reconstruction that is necessary afterwards makes it seem more like an occupation. Of the three houses located in Chicago, Cleveland, and Macon—for you Yanks, that's in Georgia—just one house has three bathrooms, the others only have two. Let's do the math: three sisters, three spouses, and four kids equals ten people divided by two bathrooms equals disaster.

Not only do we lack sufficient plumbing for these occupations, but again, the house in Cleveland is the only one with more than two bedrooms. Let's see, ten people divided by two bedrooms equals 0.001 feet of private space.

Not good.

Besides all the proximity issues, the kids want to follow you around and every other second or so ask, "What are you doing?" After an answer is provided, the next ten questions are all one word: "Why?"

But I've figured out how to beat this surefire recipe for insanity. I escape. I get outside the host house by myself. I go running.

The beauty of my plan is that some of the people in the family view running as torture, so there's no way they'll come with me. Unfortunately, most are dynamic; they change as time marches on. Two of the adults have recently co-opted my strategy and have begun running themselves. That's okay, I'm dynamic, too; sometimes I whisper to my wife, "I'm going running," and then I sneak out the back door. Other times, when invited to go for a run, I'll decline with some made-up excuse. My wife would say a poorly made-up excuse, but that's not the point. All I care about is that the excuse works. Then I can go for a run by myself later on, having miraculously recovered from whatever ailment afflicted me for an hour or two. I don't worry about hard feelings because I'm sure the only reason the other person invited me along is because he or she got caught trying to sneak out the back door.

An even better way to find isolation when the family is around is to do the menial or gross tasks that no one else wants to do. Whenever I find that I'm overwhelmed, I like to go outside and pick up the dog doo-doo. Well, maybe "like" is the wrong word, but this trick works like a charm. Cleaning the yard is such a hated task at the house in Cleveland that I'm starting to think that they leave all those land mines out there just for me and my periodic visits. When I grab a plastic bag and head into the yard, it's as if I were playing a game of hide-and-seek, and I'm the seeker. Suddenly, everyone else has vanished. The house is instantly empty—or so it seems. Interestingly enough, as soon as I've finished the wretched task, they all reappear.

No dog? Try taking out the garbage. You don't have to slip out the back door to do this one alone. Indeed, you can shout at the top of your lungs, "Hey! I'm going to take all the garbage out to the street [or wherever], who wants to party with me!" Besides wielding the aforementioned heavy-duty plastic bag full of doo-doo, there's no better way to find yourself alone.

I've recently noticed that even the nonrunners are beginning to copy my tricks. When Brenda sees that her kids are within strangling distance of an "adult," she'll scamper off to the spa for a facial or a massage. Donna likes to go on coffee runs for everyone. Sam smokes a stogie—pretty much guaranteeing isolation.

So if you're like me and you place great value on time spent alone, yet you belong to a tight-knit family that periodically mobilizes the troops and invades your home, don't forget that the best way to find seclusion is in those activities in which no one else wants to participate. Or, more precisely, no one wants to hang out with you when you're carrying a big bag of poop around. That one works even if the household doesn't own a dog.

SURVIVAL HINTS

1. If you need alone time, volunteer to clean up the yard.
2. You can also have a break by walking the dog, if one is available.
3. Take out the garbage without being asked.

4. Sneak out and buy coffee for everyone as a surprise for your hosts.
5. Do some spontaneous food shopping when you need a break.
6. When too much togetherness gets to you, go for a run or a walk.

Murray's Big Surprise

Irving Schwartz

ABOUT FIFTEEN YEARS AGO, when my son Mike decided to transfer from his college, located in a bad neighborhood of Philadelphia, to a smaller one in rural Pennsylvania, I was delighted. As we eagerly anticipated taking him to his new school for the fall semester, some seven hours from home, I looked at a map and saw that it was halfway to Indiana, where my brother Murray had moved a few years earlier.

The middle child of three, Murray had never married, was always a carefree single guy who took nice vacations and always owned a new car. He'd always been my kids' favorite uncle, quick to laugh and joke, and the life of every gathering. When he moved, everyone missed him terribly, and I thought it would be fun to make the trip and see him, especially because we'd be half way there after taking Mike to his new school. And once we were sure he'd be in town, we'd make it a surprise visit.

So I called Murray to say hello, mentioned that we were taking Mike to college, and asked what he'd been up to. "Any trips coming up?" I asked, "I know you're always traveling for your job." Naturally, I wanted to make sure he'd be home.

Murray, sounding tired, said, "Yeah, I've been to Chicago a few times this month, but I'm going to be here for the next few weeks, at least until I get bored and think up a reason to go see a client out of town."

"Well, I have to be going, Mur. We've got to get Mike packed up for his new school year, and it always takes forever to pack the Explorer. Plus the kid insists on taking everything he owns except his bedroom furniture. Anyway, maybe sometime we'll come out and see you on one of these trips, but it'd be a really long ride."

Murray sighed. "Yeah, we'll have to plan it someday," he said without enthusiasm. "Maybe we could meet halfway sometime," he added quickly.

I kept wondering whether something was wrong, but figured he was probably just tired from all his trips. I thought, perhaps even a bit enviously, that maybe ole

Murray was having a little too much fun on the road at all those trade shows.

The day of our departure arrived and off we went to Mike's new school. After dropping him off, we stayed overnight in the middle of nowhere; this wasn't the hottest of spots my kid had picked, out there in Podunk, and we were happy to be on our way to Indianapolis. At least it was a city. There's nothing I like less than being stuck out in the sticks with no diners, restaurants, or movie theaters, all of which I consider the minimum requirements for habitation.

Indianapolis was about another ten hours from the college, a long and boring trip, not to mention flat, and we were glad finally to check in at our hotel. Our SUV was relatively new, and the ride had been comfortable, despite the numerous trucks zooming along the interstate.

I called Murray and told him we were in a hotel in Indianapolis. He coughed, or should I say choked, and finally gasped, "You're here, in Indiana?" "Yep." I said. "Right here. I can see the dome of the stadium where the Colts play."

"You're not kidding around, are you, Irv? You're really here?" Murray sounded kind of faint, as if he were underwater with a bowling ball in his stomach. I'd even have to say that he sounded as if he might be turning green.

Finally, after some shocked sputters of attempted conversation, Murray asked us to come over to his place for coffee and cake.

Murray's directions were pretty good, except for the three wrong turns and the dead-end street after the two detours. We had to stop at three gas stations for directions. You'd have thought he *wanted* us to get lost. But what the heck, he was still relatively new in town and probably didn't know his way around that well yet, and maybe he didn't come this way very often.

We finally pulled into Murray's driveway, where we were surprised to see bicycles lying next to a basketball hoop near the garage. We thought it was a little odd; being your basic nearsighted Jewish accountant with a slouch and two bad knees, Murray wasn't much of an athlete. But maybe the previous owners had kids who played basketball, or maybe the kids next door were a little careless with their bikes.

We rang the front door bell. First, a fluffy little black dog bounded to the door, growling and barking at the predators on the porch. We were surprised because Murray had never mentioned that he now owned a dog. My brother usually called me from work, so I wouldn't have heard the dog barking. Irving pulled the bouncing fur noise maker away and welcomed us in.

And that's when the real surprises began—for us.

Murray called out, "Danny, Eric, Mark, come on in here please and meet your aunt and uncle."

Into the room shuffled a boy of around seven, followed by another one who was ten or eleven. Next, a lanky teenager slouched into the room; he was wearing baggy shorts and regulation basketball shoes and hugged a basketball under one arm.

"Well," I thought, "that explains the bikes and the basketball hoop. But what the heck, did he say aunt and uncle?!"

We stood there blinking, our eyebrows practically reaching around to the backs of our necks, our eyes popping and our jaws to our knees. What the heck was going on, and who were these kids?

My first thought was that maybe Murray had "adopted" some kids from the neighborhood, or was a Big Brother, or had taken in foster kids, none of which seemed to fit with his carefree bachelor lifestyle. Besides, he'd never said a thing about it.

We didn't know what to do, so we smiled and said, "Hello."

Then Murray called out, "Edie, will you please come in and meet your in-laws?"

That was when a dark-haired, roundish woman appeared, a tentative smile on her face. "Nice to meet you. I've heard so much about you," she said shyly and in a half whisper.

Finally, after the kids had stood squirming for a while, the oldest said, “Dad, I need to practice my jump shot before dark.” Murray told them they could all go back outside.

“I don’t know how to tell you this,” Murray coughed out, clearing his throat enough times to have totally removed most of the top layer of skin. “Edie and I have been together for fifteen years. When she became pregnant with our oldest boy, Mark, we were embarrassed because we weren’t married yet, and you know how old-fashioned Mother and Dad were, so we kind of kept things a secret.”

After a bit more throat clearing, choking, and a bit of gasping, he went on: “After a while, it got too complicated to come clean, and that’s why I finally moved out here with the family after Mother and Dad finally passed on. I know I should have told everyone a long time ago, but it just got too hard, I was in too deep, and I was a coward. I hope you can understand and forgive me.”

We stood there speechless for a minute, and then I found my voice: “There’s nothing to forgive, Murray.” I told him. “I’m sure you did what you thought was right. And you have a beautiful family. It’s great, a wonderful surprise. And the boys all look just like you and me when we were kids!”

Murray breathed a sigh of relief, and we all sat down for dessert.

"So, Murray," I asked, "What was with those directions? We were zigging and zagging, making U-turns and detours. Don't you know where you're going out here yet? Or were you trying to lose us permanently?"

Everyone laughed and dug into Edith's blueberry cake.

My wife and I had a lot to talk about on the long drive home.

SURVIVAL HINTS

1. Never, ever pay surprise visits to out of town relatives, even close ones.
2. Reserve judgment on all exposed family secrets—you can't ever really know why whatever happened did, and you'd want the same response yourself.
3. Go with the flow, and don't let things throw you too much. Whatever it is, you'll get used to it.
4. Unless someone has been seriously damaged or harmed, accept what you find out: you can't change it and it's not up to you anyway.

Humidity Hell

Evelyn M. Fazio

I'VE NEVER BEEN A big fan of Florida. But there's a reason for this. When I was about five years old, my grandparents moved to Miami. The following June, my parents took me out of school early so that we could go down to visit the grandparents before things got too hot. But we were too late. It's already too hot for human life in Miami in June. At least, that's how it seemed to me. But we were neophytes, and had no idea what awaited us.

So we boarded the plane and I'm happy to report that I enjoyed my first plane trip very much, from looking into the cockpit to running around the cabin and watching the flight attendants go about their busy routines. It was all great fun. That is, until we landed in Miami and they opened the door of the plane.

The minute the ten-ton wet blanket of humid air hit me in my air-conditioned little face, I thought I would suffocate and fall head-first down the staircase onto the tarmac. Because I was small, I was first in line to go out the door and down the steps; but that damp unbreathable air made me turn to my father, who was standing directly behind me, already sweating, and ask: "Do Grandma and Grandpa have air conditioning?"

"No," he replied.

"Can we go home?" I asked, hopefully.

"Are you kidding? We just flew all the way down here. Come on, let's get going!" He laughed and rolled his eyes at my mother.

So off we went, into the hellish humidity of late June Miami. Ugh. Just remembering it almost makes me swoon. The air was so laden with moisture you could practically roll it up into a ball—it was that thick and heavy. It could have been a new Olympic sport—the humidity ball toss.

We arrived at Grandma and Grandpa's little bungalow in the early afternoon. The clouds were heavy and low, and soon lightning was flashing across the greenish and darkening sky, but we were so happy to be together again that we didn't pay attention to the weather.

That night, as we sat stuffed in front of the tiny black-and-white television, its rabbit-ear antennas perched on top, we learned that an enormous hurricane, the first one of the season, was heading straight for Miami. The weather guy pointed right at our part of town, and we exchanged raised-eyebrow looks.

"Hmmm," we all thought. "What great timing for our visit!"

Being a child, I wasn't too concerned. I was with my family—so what could happen? I was relieved that it had cooled down a little since sunset, and the wind had picked up a bit, but it was still way too hot for me.

When nobody was looking, I would go into the kitchen and stick my head inside the refrigerator to breathe the wonderfully cool and decent air for a few minutes—that is, until someone came into the kitchen, which was often. So my cool-air breaks were all too brief, and they only made going back to the hot humid dampness even worse. Not only that, but the grownups kept asking me whether I was still hungry or wanted a drink, and I would just shrug and say, "No, not really," and move to another room, desperate for a breeze, a gust, something, anything. But there was nothing. Not anywhere in Miami, except inside that fridge and in my beloved and longed-for icy cold airplane.

We went to bed that night in happy anticipation of all the adventures that our week in Florida promised, especially trips to the Seaquarium, Parrot Jungle, and

Key Biscayne, as well as the beach and the relative cool of the ocean.

During the night, the hurricane descended noisily on our humid little part of Miami, but luckily our part of town emerged unscathed. We learned later that shortly after the hurricane had passed over us a tornado had touched down a few blocks away—the first ever recorded in Miami—and had taken out a whole section of the neighborhood next to ours. While we slept, the funnel had passed right over us, and it could have peeled off our tiny roof! But did it blow away the heat and mugginess? Nope.

Despite making a mess, the hurricane did not cool things off, nor did it dehumidify the air. The wet blanket just continued on and on; every activity became a chore, no matter how much fun it was supposed to be.

As we ran around to tourist attractions, we exhausted ourselves with each immersion into the sauna-like air, and almost every activity naturally took place outdoors.

Not only that, but we didn't spend much time at the beach; my grandparents' section of Miami wasn't even close to it on the map! I kept thinking that this isn't what they told me about when they said we were going to Florida. "Where's the water?" I kept wondering. At least you can't feel humidity under water. And there are breezes on the ocean, even in Miami. But alas, we only got there a few times.

Meanwhile, back at the bungalow, I spent a lot of time in the garage, which provided some shelter from the relentless sun, and once in a while the air moved a little, making it cooler than inside the house. It was still humid, but didn't seem as bad as it felt inside the tiny house. I didn't stay there long, though, because lizards also liked the shady breezes.

I tried to distract myself from the disgusting heat and mugginess by watching my grandfather calling and feeding his cardinals, who not only answered him but ate right out of his hand. "Come'n down," he'd call, and they'd swoop in like little planes responding to the control tower at Miami International. I was glad they were flying around, because at least I got a breeze once in a while from their flapping wings. Now that's a kid who was desperate for any kind of moving air!

After a week in Humidity Hell, it was finally time to go home. Despite being sorry about having to say good-bye to my grandparents, I could barely wait to be sealed into that ice-cold airplane, not to mention my gleeful anticipation of the air conditioning that awaited us at home.

Finally, we took off, and for the first time in a week I could actually breathe without the seven thousand pounds of barometric pressure on my chest. For the only recorded instance of my young life, I was actually looking forward to winter!

SURVIVAL HINTS

1. Check out the climate before agreeing to visit anybody, especially for your vacation.
2. Try to make sure you go to Florida in the winter instead of late June.
3. Don't stand in front of the refrigerator with the door open—it makes the milk go sour!

No Frills!

Ginny Chandoha

SOME RELATIVES, especially the single females, seem to revel in their femininity. My husband refers to it as "girly stuff." Personally, I am not a collector, and I don't relish frilly things, so I am happy when we visit my single female relatives: My husband has to endure the "girly stuff" for a few days, and it makes him appreciate me that much more.

I have one relative, Arlene, who is a serial collector; her obsession changes as new collectibles tickle her fancy. As a result, her house is crammed with things. Dolls fill every couch and chair. Enough pillows for a half dozen people to sleep in the bed. Shams are a mystery to my husband; dust ruffles were, too, until I explained that they hide everything stashed under the bed.

My husband almost fainted the minute he laid eyes on the bathroom. It was tiny, just like the rest of the house, and was it filled with baskets of potpourri and fancy soaps. There was no place for him to put his toothbrush and his shaving paraphernalia. From the ceiling dangled baskets of dusty imitation ivy. The bathroom wallpaper was busy with zillions of tiny flowers. The bathtub covered by a flowery curtain complete with a frilly valance. The most amazing part was when my husband pulled the curtain aside to step into the shower and slammed his foot against the clear glass shower door hiding behind the curtain. There was barely room between the toilet and tub, and to add insult to injury, one had to step over a ceramic fawn that was kneeling on the floor. So many fancy hand towels filled the one rack that there was no place to hang the washcloths or bath towels. "Too much girly stuff!" he'd complain to me.

However, it was in Arlene's house that I learned an important lesson about a man's perspective on bathroom fixtures. Something that most women, especially unattached ones, probably never realize. It was a revelation for me as well, but more so for my husband. As I mentioned earlier, I'm a streamlined individual, and

I don't dress the bathroom fixtures. Arlene had covered not just the toilet lid but also the tank.

Being a woman, I had never realized that toilet covers prevent the lid and seat from staying up by themselves. A man has to hold the lid and seat up with one knee, hold his clothing aside, and attempt to urinate in the correct spot. And he knows he'll catch hell if he misses! Quite a juggling act, one that requires three hands. The last straw came when, as he reached to flush, the lid slammed down and hit him in the sensitive private parts.

The next time we visit, we'll be staying at a motel.

SURVIVAL HINTS

1. Remember that you have to respect a host's style, but you do not have to like it.
2. Always check to see what's behind the curtain!
3. If you have to, by all means check into a hotel if the clutter and frills get to you!

California-Bound

Anna Jane Grossman

WHEN I WAS TWENTY-TWO, I dated a handful of interesting men. There was John-the-Rock-Climber, Dave-the-Private-Eye, Jesse-the-Parachutist, and Phil-the-Rocket Scientist.

And then there was Mike Jones.

Mike Jones would never be Mike or Michael or M to me. He was Mike Jones. Indeed, his last name was his most defining characteristic. There were a few days when he wore a beard, and I was hopeful that he could be bearded-Mike. But then he shaved it off.

Sure, Mike Jones had his interests. At first I tried to refer to them when describing him to my friends. "I'm dating this guy Mike—he's a twenty-nine-year-old aspiring yoga teacher," I'd say. "He's also really into Kabala." But this was just embarrassing. He was better off just being Mike Jones.

I first met Mike Jones in a Manhattan creative writing class in which he wrote a lot about his family. He wrote about how, when he was in high school, his dad would charge his teenage friends for gas when he drove them to soccer practice. He wrote about how his mom ate only uncooked foods.

The first day we met, Mike Jones showed me an issue of *Rolling Stone* he had stuffed in his backpack. In it was a spread on a popular all-girl hard rock band. "My sister is in this group!" he said. "Oh, yeah, right," I said. I pointed to the saddest-looking of them all—an overweight and sullen teen holding a bass. It wasn't that she looked as if she was contemplating suicide; rather, she looked as if she'd already swallowed a bottle of Tylenol and was just waiting for it to take effect. "That's probably her," I said, mockingly. "How did you know?" he said.

Mike Jones always calculated exactly how much I owed him after a meal. Mike Jones always walked a few paces ahead of me. Mike Jones wore patchouli.

So it's no great wonder that I didn't particularly like dating Mike Jones. But dating him seemed unavoidable because every time I tried to break up with him those first few weeks, he'd cry. Somehow, having sex with a cheap man who bored me seemed easier than drying his tears and eating alone.

But in Mike Jones's mind, things seemed to be going swimmingly. "Can I ask you something," he whispered to me in bed a month after we had met. "Would you take my name if we got married?"

I shouldn't have been surprised when Mike Jones became obsessed with the idea of meeting my family, all of whom lived within four blocks of me. But I didn't really see the point; I didn't think he'd be around long enough for it to be worth making the introduction. I told him they were traveling. I told him they were sick.

When he tired of my excuses, he decided that I should meet his family in California. His mom was a writing teacher, and he'd told her all about me, he said. He'd even sent her a short story I'd written. Three days later, I received a critique of it by email. "B+," she'd written at the end.

The following week, when I arrived at his apartment, he announced he had something to show me. He brought me to his computer and sat me down in front of it. "Oh, she's so cute!" the computer squeaked.

"That's my mom!" Mike said. "I set up a computer video phone!" But it was working only in one direction.

"Hi, Mrs. Jones," I said, waving at the blank screen and forcing a smile. "Mikey? She's adorable!" it said. "Is she Jewish?"

That night, Mike Jones announced that he wanted me to go with him to the suburbs of San Francisco to meet his parents and his sister in person. I told him I couldn't; I had a dentist appointment I needed to prepare for. Next thing I knew, my lap was wet with his tears; by midnight, he was entering my credit card number on Priceline.com.

"My mom wants to know if you eat tempeh," Mike Jones said in the cab on the way to LaGuardia. It was raining and we were stuck in traffic. I was daydreaming about California. I focused on how nice it would be to sit on the beach. I was imagining myself tan. "*Do* you eat tempeh?"

Our flight from LaGuardia was to leave at 4:00 p.m., but it was already 3:30 p.m. and we hadn't even entered Queens yet. It was pouring; the windshield wipers were pounding. "You know, I think we might miss this flight," I said, trying to sound concerned.

Alas, we didn't miss it. The flight had been delayed, just my luck. We boarded around 7:00 p.m., and then sat in the plane in the middle of the tarmac for the next two hours. Still on the ground, the cabin swayed from side to side, rocking to the beat of the storm.

As we approached hour three of taxiing, I started to consider the possibility of getting off the plane somehow. Would I have to fake a medical emergency to get off at this point? Would Mike Jones go with me, or would he want to take his chances in the storm?

"I feel like we're going to die and we haven't even taken off yet," I said to him.

I longed to be told that it was all going to be okay. Instead, he pulled out a prayer book and started muttering words in Hebrew. "It's the prayer you say when you're about to die," he said. We still had not even left the ground.

He then got on the phone and spent an hour talking to his mom. The conversation ended when the flight attendant told him we were about to take off.

I've never been a frightened flyer. During the mild moments of fear I've experienced, I have reminded myself of comforting "facts": More people die in bathtubs than in planes, and once you are above the clouds, all weather is perfect weather for flying. But I can now say with authority that whether you're above the clouds or beneath them, from the window seat of a plane, every bolt of lightning appears close enough to hit you. I'm certain I was not the only passenger in tears.

This is it, I thought. This is how I'm going to die. I'm going to meet my end at the age of twenty-two while sitting next to a guy whom I think I might actually hate.

Suddenly, I could vividly imagine our memorial service. It would be done as a joint affair, and would probably be held at the Kabala Centre. His sullen sister's band would perform. Rumors that he'd been getting ready to propose to me in California would be flying through the rows of folding chairs. My parents and the Joneses would embrace each other and comfort each other and tell each other that at least we were in each others' arms for those final, lightning-zapped moments. A tree with both our names on it would be planted in Israel. Strangers would pass by it and imagine us as tragic lovers who'd met their end together. The Joneses would ask my parents to pay more towards the plaque that would be on the tree because my name has more letters than his.

But then a miracle occurred: We landed.

The good news was that we were safe on land again; the bad news was that we were laying over in Pittsburgh. The worse news was that because of delays all over the eastern seaboard, our connecting flight had been rescheduled and wouldn't leave until the following evening. "I've never seen it this bad in eight years of working in airports," the woman at the Delta information desk told me. "And the rain? Much more dangerous than flying in snow!"

"Is it going to rain tomorrow, too?" I asked hopefully. "Yup," she said. Then she told us that the airport hotel was completely booked and Delta wouldn't be covering the cost of a room.

At around 1:00 a.m., we finally found a clean-enough motel with vacancies twenty minutes from the airport.

We got milkshakes from the Denny's across the highway, and then I fell onto the bed.

Mike lay down next to me and called his mom. He insisted that I say hello to her. Her voice was like honey laced with Splenda. "You having fun? You taking good care of my boy? Can't wait to meet you! Did you know Mikey is turning thirty next month? Find out for me what he wants for his special day, okay?" I passed the phone back to Mike Jones, and I could hear her screeching on the other end as he explained exactly what had happened.

"What?" she said. "You tell them you need to be here tomorrow morning, not tomorrow night! Mikey! Are you listening to me? Then fine, I'll call the airline and tell them they need to get their act together, damn it! Mikey, why are you such a wimp about this? Tell them there is no way you can wait for an evening flight. Okay, Mikey?" He hung up and grinned broadly. "My mom is going to call the airline and yell at them for us," he said, beaming. "And she said she'd pay for the motel!" She called back half an hour later to inform us she'd persuaded the airlines to book us on a 6:00 a.m. flight.

By the time we went bed, it was after 2:00 a.m. and it was still thundering. All I could think about were all the other places in the world where I could be at that moment. Mike Jones was curled up, his back towards me.

"You know what?" I said softly. He grunted. "I think I can't do this. It's all just too much for me." "Huh?" he said. And then he was snoring.

"Mikey? Are you awake? It's wakey time!" I could hear Mrs. Jones's voice through the cell phone again when she called to get us up at 5:00 a.m. She called again an hour later to make sure that we'd made it to the airport with time to spare. But she was off the line by the time we approached the ticket counter together to pick up our boarding passes.

"We're going to San Francisco," I told the white-haired agent, as I picked sleep out of my eyes. But then, lightning finally struck me for real. "Actually, he's going to San Francisco. I need a ticket back to New York."

I wish I could say it was the first time I saw Mike Jones cry. It was, however, the first time I'd heard him yelp or yell. But it didn't last long. He stormed off in a huff as the agent printed up my new ticket.

Once he was out of sight, he called my cell phone from the other side of the airport, but I couldn't understand what he was saying through the sniffling. "I'm sorry," was all I could offer. "I'm sorry, I just can't. I couldn't." And then I, too, started to weep.

Not long after he hung up, he was back near the ticket counter, where I was clutching my new flight itinerary. His tears appeared to have dried somewhat.

"How could you do this to me," he kept saying. "How could you?" My only response was another "sorry" whispered through a wall of tears. "I thought I loved you," he said. "But now I'm sorry we ever met." He then turned on his heel and walked stoically into McDonald's.

That was the last I ever saw of Mike Jones . . . well, almost. Six months later, when I heard him call my name, I was waiting for my mom outside the Barnes & Noble near Union Square; it had been drizzling earlier in the day, and I still had the hood of my raincoat up—I couldn't believe he'd seen me. "Hi," I said, forcing a smile.

He looked at me mournfully, and I felt as if we were in a movie; except this was *his* movie. I'd walk away, but the focus would stay on him. I asked him how the trip to California had worked out. He told me it went well.

"Everyone felt so sorry for poor Mikey, being left by his girl in the airport," he said. "So I got tons of really cool presents. Oh, and my sister's band wrote a song about how much you suck." Just then, Mom came out. I introduced them, but when Mom offered her hand, Mike Jones skulked away. "Who was that?" she asked.

"Mike Jones," I said. No recognition registered on her face. "Mike, the-guy-I-was-supposed-to-go-to-California-with-but-chickened-out," I said.

And, at last, he had a full name.

SURVIVAL HINTS

1. Be sure you really want to take that trip to visit someone else's family before you agree to go. Better to assert oneself early and avoid drama, embarrassment, and disappointment later. It's also easier on the prospective hosts to decline right away, before too much planning has been done.
2. Try to avoid meeting a date's family until you are sure of your feelings about the person in question; this way, you'll spare everyone's feelings and stay sane yourself.

You Can Go Home Again

Flint Wainess

MY MOTHER HASN'T TOUCHED my bedroom since I was sixteen, which I take as a sign that she believes I will be such a horrific failure in life that I will be moving back in some day soon. Since I moved out of the house twelve years ago, she has redone all three bathrooms, the living room, her bedroom, the backyard, the deck (twice), and the kitchen (three times). She even remodeled my father out of the house a few years ago. So there is no explanation for her failure to overhaul my small white room with my signed Bar Mitzvah cutout on the wall other than to say: *You were my first born and I love you, but let's face it, adulthood hasn't worked out so well for you. And, because you are too stubborn to work at the Gap, you will have to move back into your bedroom and live with your mother, which will be as unpleasant for me as it will be for you.*

I live in Los Angeles, where I don't quite make a living as a writer (it's humiliating enough being a sit-com writer; imagine the humiliation of being an unemployed sit-com writer), and I try to come home to Birmingham—Michigan, not Alabama—once or twice a year, because if I don't my parents will disown me and refuse to let me move back in after I do fail as an adult. The key is to maximize these visits (e.g., come home on a weekend when there's a Michigan football game, the Cider Mill is open, and I can play a round of golf but avoid seeing cousins, grandparents, and other assorted relatives and hangers-on).

It's not that I don't like my parents or my hometown. I love my parents. They were the cool parents. In high school, when I smoked cigarettes at Olga's Kitchen or stole beer from the neighborhood garages, one of my friends would invariably call my folks and rat me out (apparently they liked hanging out with my parents more than they liked hanging out with me). We would fight like hell in those days, but it always had a theatrical quality to it, as if we were going through the motions of what parents and teens were supposed to do. There was a tacit understanding that all would work out in the end, that one day we would laugh about my booming business of taking other people's SATs for money.

My family has its oddballs, one being my late Uncle Marvin, a successful doctor who was also a deeply troubled kleptomaniac; after he died, we never had to buy toilet paper or tissues or towels again. But, for the most part, we've always been the Jewish version of *Leave It to Beaver:* loud and crass but also loving and stable. My parents were always the couple that other couples emulated, that *I* emulated. Coming home for visits was great because we would go to fancy dinners and sporting events, and when we weren't doing the things I enjoyed I could try to hook up with old girlfriends who still lived in town, or I could lock myself in the basement and play pool while blasting my old "Whitesnake" albums.

But a little over five years ago, everything changed: My parents suddenly and inexplicably divorced. Suddenly, like a scene from *Star Wars,* every second of my visits was imbued with great meaning, and great conflict. Suddenly, staying sane was like watching Jar Jar Binks: a nearly impossible challenge.

"Where should we go for dinner?"

My mother the schoolteacher asks this while I'm in the bathroom. I've never considered this an optimal time for conversation, but my parents have always viewed these moments—when I'm trapped and can't move—as an ideal time to begin talking to me.

"I'm in the bathroom," I yell, stating the obvious.

My mother goes quiet, but now my bathroom ritual has been interrupted. My plumbing is fickle; it will be backed up for days.

After doing nothing in the bathroom for a long time, I head through the remodeled hall and into my mother's bedroom. I am struck by the deeply disturbing thought that a strange man (or strange men) might have slept in this bed with her, the same bed she had shared with my father for thirty years. My mom starts to speak, but I quickly run out of the bedroom. As I look around the house, I am aware that I lived in this house for eighteen years, that I've walked this same hall countless thousands of times, and yet it all feels like a dream. Is this the spot where my father threw me against the wall after my mother refused to go to my high school graduation because I wouldn't shave? Is this really the room where my mother tossed a cold cup of coffee at me after I admitted to stealing the class ring of a rich kid from school and selling it at a pawn shop in downtown Detroit? (The coffee missed me, and instead stained my mom's favorite couch.)

I turn on the television. My mother turns it off. She wants to know whether I flew all the way across country to watch *Three's Company* reruns.

This is followed by a long, unhealthy dose of silence.

"So . . . "

"So . . . how are you?" she asks, in the same way she asks every time she calls; if I start to answer in depth, she becomes bored and says, "Okay, I was just calling to say hi." With my father and brother, spending time together is easy because we enjoy sports. All awkward pauses can be filled with a passionate discussion regarding reports on the Michigan football team's new offensive line, or the Tigers' pitching staff. But with my mother, I can never think of small talk.

"Will you get a haircut while you're here?" Mom asks.

"Probably not."

She reacts as if I had just jabbed her in the eye with my high school yearbook. "Will you at least shave then?"

"I don't know."

"You could use some new pants."

I wait for the *you look like a hobo speech* to end, but that doesn't seem likely. I consider pointing out that "poor Anne Frank didn't have the luxury of worrying about whether to shave, or whether her jeans fit."

This is a variation on a line I had been using for years. Whenever my parents fret about something superficial, I remind them of Anne Frank. It's a pretty cheap tactic, using Anne Frank to make my parents feel shallow, but it's also pretty effective.

Fortunately, my mother gets sick of me before I can provoke a fight by trotting out Anne Frank. "You're three times seven," she says. "Do what you want."

I'm actually three times seven plus nine, and later my mom hands me a razor and tells me I have a hair appointment for the next morning, but at least her heart is in the right place.

An hour later, I'm lying in bed watching a fairly brilliant episode of *Duck Tales* when my mother enters. She hands me the wedding announcements from the *Jewish News*.

"Jodi Price is getting married." This is supposed to be a provocative comment, a veiled way of saying "Why aren't you getting married?" But one of the keys to staying sane is not taking the bait. At some point, the child is required to be more mature than the parent.

"Let's eat in Birmingham, maybe Middle-Eastern," I say, while all the clocks in the McDuck mansion are being changed to Saturday as part of an evil plot against Scrooge.

"Isn't your father always in Birmingham?" asks my mother. My father the dentist was somehow given Birmingham in the divorce. Although it was my mother the teacher who did the divorcing, it is my father who takes the blame (not for having a girlfriend *while* he was married, but for having one after). "He's probably with Marylyn," says my mother. "You know, she would just love to marry a rich dentist to take care of those three kids of hers."

My mother then suggests eating at The Beverly Hills Grille because she always suggests The Beverly Hills Grille. Apparently, an extremely short, almost midget, person whom I was briefly friends with in middle school works there, and my mother thinks it would be thrilling for both of us if he poured me some wine. I pass, because I have been informed that the Almost Midget Person Whom I Was Briefly Friends With in Middle School has a baby, which means he will want to show me pictures of this Midget Spawn Baby on his cell phone. There's a chance that he will have pictures of his dog as well, and, as badly as I yearn for distractions while eating with my mother, I do not want to see anyone's dog or baby on a camera phone (if you really love the dog and baby so goddamn much, buy a real camera). Also, I think it's pretty strange that my mom and dad used to go to The Grille together all the time. She doesn't want to have dinner with my father, but she wants to go to the place they used to go as a couple three times a week?

The phone rings; it's my father. "Where are we going for dinner," he asks.

"I'm going to have dinner with Mom," I say.

"With your mother?"

"Yes. Your ex-wife, my mother. She's a special lady."

"But you're leaving tomorrow."

"I saw you yesterday."

"You're not home that often. I thought we would have dinner together."

"I'll come by after dinner."

"You don't have a car."

"You can't drive my car," yells my mother. I don't know how she heard what my father said into the phone, but perhaps this is a skill learned from years as a schoolteacher.

"I can't drive her car," I repeat. "Why don't we all just have dinner?"

This is not a scene from *The Parent Trap*. I do not have a secret plan to put the band back together. I just want to eat, and I want to eat with my parents.

"Mom," I ask, "can Dad come to dinner?"

She pauses for a long time. "I don't think his girlfriend will like that."

My father meets us at the restaurant. He and my mom don't kiss or hug. Part of me wants desperately to push them together, to scream, "Don't you see you're going to end up alone, living in Boca Raton?" But part of me is fascinated by the inexorable humanness of my parents.

The three of us settle uncomfortably into shiny booths, bury our faces in long menus. The first few minutes are awkward. But before I can make any obnoxious remarks, the two of them are walking down memory lane and I'm eating too much bread with too many olives in it. When I was little, I thought of my parents as stable, simple suburbanites, people who knew what they wanted and had achieved it. But as I watch them, I see how complicated their lives have been: They fell in love, found the dream; they fell out of love, lost the dream; they're still in love, they're divorced, they're dating other people, and yet they are still very much married, always will be.

"Isn't this cute," I say, "it's like we're a real family."

They ignore my comment, and my mother unexpectedly laughs at something my father says. What could it be? Damn it, don't you know you're divorced?! Then they are interrupted by two visitors: a blonde and a brunette. The blonde is staring at my father accusingly.

"Well, hello," she finally says. "I didn't know you were eating *here*."

"Well, hello," says the blonde. She appears to be in her thirties, almost pretty in a desperate housewife sort of way.

My father is beginning to turn blood white (I had heard of blood red, but this was my first experience with blood white). I wonder whether he had taken his blood pressure medication. "Um. Oh, um, hi," says my dad.

"Hi, Marylyn," says my mom to the blonde, and that's when I realize that this is my father's girlfriend.

Marylyn looks back and forth between my mother and father. It's my mother, oddly, who fills the dead air. As she and the new girl are both teachers, my mom asks a few pointed questions about the school year. Marylyn responds, but no one is really listening.

"What's good here," I say, both trying to break the tension and trying to decide what to eat.

After recommending the risotto, Marylyn and her girlfriend hesitate, then take their seats on the opposite side of the restaurant. Before leaving, Marylyn waits for what seems like an eternity for my father to say something important, to explain why he's eating and laughing with his ex-wife. He doesn't.

"Your girlfriend was checking up on you," my mother says immediately.

My father shifts in the booth. "No she wasn't. She didn't know we were coming here."

"That's a big coincidence, don't you think?" says my mom.

"No, I don't."

"Are you going to marry her? Because a thirty-five-year-old woman with three kids isn't dating for fun."

This is a pretty good point, but I'm trying not to take sides.

"I'm not having this conversation," says my dad, and, thankfully, he's not. I feel sick from all the bread, and we're not even up to the salads.

During dinner, my parents ignore the pink elephant in the room and instead turn their mixed-up emotions to me.

"Your father and I have been talking," says my mother, "and we've decided that if you go back to graduate school and finish your PhD, we will support you. Financially." *Wait. They were talking. When? On the phone? And, if so, who called whom?*

"Thank you, but I left graduate school because I hated it," I say.

"You spent three years there," interjects my mother, "why can't you just finish?"

"Because it would take two more years of my life, at least, and I would like not to waste two years pursuing something I'm not interested in."

"Where I'm from, when you start something, you finish it."

"We're from the same place. I'm from your house."

My parents exchange concerned glances. When I was little and we fought, I would yell, "Get a divorce!" Now I wanted to yell, "I can't believe you took my advice!"

"Did you know my brother went to law school at thirty?" asks my father.

"So you want me to go back to graduate school, but a *different* graduate school?"

"You don't have to practice law. As a lawyer, there are many things you can do."

"Is one of them being a writer, which is my career?"

"You're thirty. It's time to get your act together."

"Together? I am together." I neglect to mention an incident from earlier that morning when I paid one hundred and four dollars for a scone. Four dollars for the scone, using my ATM card, and a hundred dollars for the insufficient funds fee the bank charged because I had only three dollars and eighty cents in my bank account.

Out of the corner of my eye, I could see my dad's girlfriend staring us down.

Dinner goes quickly, and I've never been so thankful for speedy service. As we get up, I wait for my father to head toward Marylyn to apologize for lying about going to dinner with his ex-wife, to make a joke or two about the service. But he doesn't. My mom has to stop by a friend's house, so I leave with my dad. It's raining. We run to the car. He puts it in gear.

"So you're not serious about her?"

"What?"

"Your girlfriend. The Big Marylyn."

"I am serious about her."

"Oh, well, then you might want to go back in to the restaurant."

I really would like it if I would shut up right now, but I can't seem to make my mouth listen to my brain. "If you don't go back in," I continue, "she is going to break up with you."

"You think so?" Is my dad really this clueless? "You lied to her. She caught you. Then, instead of going over there and apologizing or saying it's no big deal, you flee. Go back in there, or you're done."

My dad stares at me for a long time. "I'll be right back." He throws his coat over his head, disappears into the rain.

Two years later, thanks to my intervention, my father and The Big Marylyn are still going strong. And my mother is doing something resembling dating with a tiny troll of a man who happens to be my father's former good friend. My parents' lives continue to be intertwined. They are friends, enemies, and, judging from the way they can still push each other's buttons, lovers. Some divorces end marriages; others are just another chapter in it.

Since the divorce, every trip has become a careful negotiation. How much time should I spend with my mom? How much time with my dad? Am I spending more quality time with one party than the other? If all the activities I want to partake in—sports, sports, and sports—favor my dad, do I have to skip them to do things I don't enjoy with my mom?

For the rest of my life, my mother will tell me to shave and get a haircut every time I see her. She'll nag me to make my bed every morning, although no one else will see it and I will just mess it up again the next day. Until I've made enough money to purchase a Malibu dream house and accepted at least three Oscars, my father will continue to hand me law school applications. I can let these things drive me nuts. I can argue and disagree with my parents at every turn. Or I can simply let the irritations wash over me.

Parents are irrational, annoying, and hypocritical; in other words, they're exactly like us. I'm lucky: Mine aren't crazy or cruel. They're decent Midwestern people who are exceptionally kind. But when I'm home with them for more than six hours, or trapped in a hotel room with them, it can be a struggle to stay sane.

Which is why, when I'm beginning to lose my temper, when I want to throw a cold cup of coffee at my mother, I remember the example of little Anne Frank, who didn't have a choice but to be trapped with her parents. They drove her crazy, but she was happy to have them.

Wedding Party

Ronda Kaysen

TO CALL MY SISTER Gina's engagement brief would be an understatement. Three weeks after she announced she was getting married, my family was gathered at the windy top of the Seattle Space Needle watching a jail judge preside over her nuptials.

This was not really a wedding, she insisted, more like a formality to keep the INS at bay. The real wedding would happen six months later, completely equipped with a white dress, a string of bridesmaids, and a drunken bachelorette party sendoff. We could refer to this affair—intended to keep her Indian boyfriend from being deported back to the third world—as a hasty engagement party.

"How many weddings does a person need?" my father asked as we sat down to eat at the Space Needle restaurant. After the September wedding, Gina and her new husband planned to meet his family in India for a third, Indian wedding. "When your mother and I got married, we didn't even hire a band. We brought our own record player and I changed the records myself," my dad said.

I had heard this version of my parents' wedding before: They drove themselves to the reception hall and my mother wore a green minidress and chunky heels. It was a very bohemian event. "When your sister wanted a custom-made dress for her senior prom, I knew I was in for it," he said.

Gina glared at my dad from across the table. The nonwedding was not going so well. Already, we had made a mess of things. My mother had left my sister's bouquet in the hotel refrigerator and my new boyfriend and I had managed make everyone late by enjoying a passionate interlude in our hotel room while we were supposed to be getting dressed.

My sister Debra's husband, a brooding New Englander named Carter, has a saying about my family. Getting us to go anywhere, he says frequently through clenched teeth, is like herding cats.

Gina, a television producer, had decided that this would be the weekend for herding. Her new husband had a friend named Faisal who owned a weekend house on Whidbey, one of the islands north of Seattle. She told us we were all invited to spend the afternoon up there, as my mother and I walked into a wedding dress shop with her on the morning after the Space Needle ceremony.

"That seems awfully far," my mother said. "I was hoping we could all just spend some time together."

"I wanted to show David Pike Place Market," I said, envisioning the remainder of my whirlwind weekend spent tooling around Seattle with my blue-eyed boyfriend.

Gina sauntered out of the dressing room draped in a cream-colored silk gown. "Whidbey will be fun," she declared. "The ferry isn't far from here at all."

Two hours later, the entire family was following Faisal in a five-car caravan through Washington state. "How did this happen?" my mother whimpered from the front seat. "This is outrageous," my father growled.

My boyfriend grimaced. I called Debra—who was one car behind my father's—on my cell phone. "We have to stop her," Debra said. "When we get to the Chevron station, we'll tell her we're turning back." I nodded vigorously, prepared for a showdown.

"You be France," Debra added. This was, after all, a month after the Iraq War started.

But at the Chevron station, our united front unraveled. My father kicked at the loose gravel. Debra looked askance and said that Evan, her two-year-old son, had diarrhea. I attempted to use Evan's illness as leverage to turn back. It was no use.

"Faisal made us lunch," Gina said. "What do you suggest we do? Just leave him?"

The Kaysen family may be a strong-willed lot, but when it comes to food, we are all of one mind. "He made lunch?" My dad perked up: "Well, that settles it."

An hour and one tense ferry ride later, we arrived at Faisal's ranch-style, beachfront house. He had forgotten to mention one key detail about the lunch. It wasn't exactly made.

As my boyfriend and I stood in the kitchen spreading butter on white bread for the cucumber sandwiches, I wondered how, exactly, we had gotten roped into making an inedible lunch for fourteen people.

My mother sulked on the sofa. My brother disappeared into an impassioned cell phone conversation. My nephew's diarrhea-induced whining devolved into a full-throttle howl. And Faisal, a boisterous, chatty fellow, seemed entirely oblivious of it all.

"George," he said, clapping my father on the back. "I must take you to see my airplane."

My father, who has about as much interest in status as he has in cucumber-and-white-bread sandwiches, cringed.

My boyfriend and I slipped out of the house for a walk along the beach. It was a chilly, early spring afternoon and the water was a steel gray. The beach was quiet and empty, sealed off from the road by stony cliffs. I had been dating David—an only child—for just a few months, but judging by the state of the rest of my family, he was by far the sanest option. "Your family's a little intense," he said.

"They're not usually this bad." I sat down on a stone boulder and glanced up at him. He looked concerned and exhausted. I realized I had thrown this poor man into the middle of my family without a life preserver.

My sister Debra came running toward us, waving her arms. "Hey, you two lovebirds, we're heading out," she said when she was within earshot. "Everyone's waiting for you." I took a deep breath and headed back to the house.

The ride back to Seattle was actually worse. Faisal dragged the caravan on a tour of the island, slowing down as we neared the private airport to make sure my father got a good view of his airplane. When we stopped in an uninspired town for no apparent reason, my mother rolled down her window and begged Faisal to take us home. He grinned and soldiered on.

We arrived back in Seattle at nearly 10:00 p.m., depleted of even the energy to complain. My flight back to New York was at 8:00 a.m. the next morning.

I still had six months to go until the *next* nonwedding.

3

When Siblings Are Rivals

Peanut Butter and Jealousy
Walter M. Heskes

The Christmas War
Sheila Myers

Brotherly and sisterly love—there is nothing quite like it. Where else can you find someone who would take your part in an argument one night and be ready to throw a pie in your face the next? They're usually there when it counts, but in between, they can really drive you nuts!

Try the following quiz to see how skilled you are at dealing with sibling rivalry, fights, disagreements, or other generalized sibling-induced mayhem.

Sanity Quiz

Your brother is coming to visit. He lives on the other side of the country. He says he is coming for only a day or two, but you know better. His day or two really means a week or two. He calls to confirm that he will be arriving early Friday morning.

Do you

A. see his number on your caller ID and not answer the phone

B. tell him you've been called out of town on business
C. make up a cot for him in the garage
D. all of the above

If you chose any of those answers, you need help coping with your siblings. The stories illustrate the concept that family is family. Despite the insanity that specific relationships can produce, some personality combinations seem almost designed to clash. Nonetheless, sibling bonds usually override everything else—sooner or later.

As you can see, some of these situations are good for a laugh in hindsight, and everyone managed to survive, so take heed of their hard-earned wisdom and sound advice!

Peanut Butter and Jealousy

Walter M. Heskes

FAT STEVIE'S FLESHY MOUTH fell open, but not for stuffing food. No, Stevie was stunned; shocked; utterly dumbfounded. In staggering disbelief, he rolled himself farther forward, balancing his roundness on the leading edge of the flimsy folding chair as it creaked unhappily under his enormous weight. His globe-like head shook from side to side, the tip of his tongue pressed the back of his lower teeth. The rough charges of air rushed in and out of his mouth; a chilling sensation crept over the back of his head as beads of gathering perspiration flooded the barren terrain of his naked scalp. Tears filled his myopic brown eyes until watery droplets fell from the tip of his nose onto his creaseless grey slacks.

"Tissue, Mr. Samuels?" the lawyer asked, pointing to the large box of Kleenex on her desk.

"Tissue?"

"No. Please," he waved at her with his free left hand. "Don't mind me. Keep going."

"You're sure?"

"Uh-huh," he nodded.

"Very well." The lawyer resumed reading his mother's will and, with each word, Stevie's heart sank lower and lower and lower.

"Esther got everything. Everything!" he thought as he boarded the late afternoon bus back to Brooklyn. Shuffling toward the rear, he found a pair of empty seats and parked himself across both. He stared down at his scuffed brown shoes. Then he glanced through the window at the passing street scenes. Finally, he closed his eyes and tried to take a nap, but he wasn't tired.

Dragging himself down the block from the bus stop, he dreaded the impending confrontation with Sammie, his fretful wife. He knew she was hoping there would be enough money for them to move out of the sparsely furnished four-room apartment they shared with their two teen-aged children, Danny and Ann. Sammie's heart was set on buying a house somewhere in Jersey.

He trudged up the long flight of stairs and found the door ajar. Inside, Sammie was standing by the stove wearing her flowery kitchen apron and matching mittens.

"How'd it go?" she called out to him.

"Um, okay, I guess," he answered, removing his jacket and hanging it in the tiny coat closet by the front door.

"What do you mean by 'Okay, *I guess*'? What does *that* mean?" Sammie sensed that something was wrong.

"She got everything, Sammie," Stevie said with calm resignation. "I got bupkiss."

"*What?* Your sister got everything? What's 'everything'? How *much* is everything?" Sammie shrieked.

"The house. The stuff in the house. The money in the bank."

"The jewelry?"

"That, too."

"Oy, vey!" Sammie cried, slapping a flowered kitchen mitten to her forehead.

"Sammie," he commanded, making a large fist with his right hand and pointing his forefinger at the ceiling, "as God is my witness, I swear I will never, *ever* have that woman in this house again. Never!"

"Which woman? Your mother or your sister?"

"Both!" he snapped. "And, if she calls, I don't want to speak to her; and if she doesn't call, I still don't want to speak to her."

"Does that mean we're not moving to Jersey?" Sammie whined.

"Yes. No Jersey." he snapped. "Now," he began, downshifting from commander to sweetie-pie, "what's for dinner? I'm starving."

"Baked ziti," she answered. "You're *still* hungry?" Sammie asked in amazement.

"Ab-so-lute-ly," Stevie declared, stretching out the word for maximum impact. "Food fixes all," he added, carefully stashing his feelings of anguish and betrayal deep into his roomy stomach. "Now, please pass me an extra large helping of that delicious-looking concoction," he said as he lowered himself into a metal folding chair at the bridge table in the breakfast nook.

Across town, sitting at the tiny kitchen table in the second-floor apartment of her mother's house—now, her own house—Esther suspected that her brother was resentful about being shut out of their mother's estate. While she was waiting for the water to boil for tea, she considered telephoning Stevie to explain why she alone deserved the sudden wealth that had been thrust upon her.

After all, she rationalized, hadn't she been the sole caretaker when their mother had become too ill to look after herself? When Stevie had married Sammie and moved to his own home, hadn't Esther continued to live in the apartment upstairs from her eccentric mother? Didn't that count for something?

The more she thought about it, the more she convinced herself that she deserved the entire estate. There were moments when she almost resented the way Stevie had abandoned his family and his relatives. Where had he been during their mother's final illness?

Tomorrow she would phone him and explain it all. But as she cut herself a thick slice of chocolate-chip pound cake, she was struck by a nasty thought. What if Stevie decided to challenge the validity of the will? They might end up in court! If that happened, all the money would go to the lawyers and everything would be lost. Now, for the first time in her life, she was afraid of her younger brother. Maybe it was better not to say anything and simply avoid the entire issue. Using her fingers, she quickly broke the willing slice of cake in half, then broke each half again and gulped down each of the delicious chunks.

Days became weeks. Weeks became months. Months became twenty-five years.

Stevie channeled his anger into a knack for relating sarcastic comments with comic timing. Esther managed her guilt by overeating.

Stevie's daughter, Hannah, had maintained contact with her cousin, Linda, who is my wife and Esther's older daughter. One day, Hannah and Linda agreed that it was time to break the silence and bring Esther and Stevie back together again.

Hannah approached her father with the idea. "For Pete's sake, Dad," Hannah argued, "how about it?"

"Who's Pete? Someone I should know?" Stevie chuckled. "Look, I never said I didn't want to see her again. She was the one who broke off with me. But, if she's had a change of heart and she wants to apologize, well, I guess that would be okay."

"Tell her she can come over here anytime she wants," Sammie added.

A few days later, Linda confronted her mother.

"Apologize?" Esther laughed. "For what?" she argued. "Stevie is the one who started this whole thing. He probably just wants money." She was silent for a moment. "Now, if he wanted to apologize to *me* for making me feel so miserable for so many years, well," she said cautiously, "maybe I might agree to see him."

Hannah told Linda that they would all meet at Stevie and Sammie's apartment the following Saturday evening at eight o'clock.

Late on Saturday afternoon, Grace, my wife's sister and Esther's other daughter, and her husband, Rob, picked up Esther at her house. It was nearly six o'clock when they arrived at our house.

"Dinner's on me," a noticeably nervous Esther volunteered. "We don't have to be at Stevie's for two hours. We have plenty of time." Esther was in no hurry to meet Stevie.

Linda suggested a bustling, noisy Italian restaurant: the perfect setting for overeating. The slow service and the large portions suited everyone.

It was just a few minutes past eight when we all arrived at Stevie and Sammie's house. Sammie answered the door. "Well, I sure hope you're hungry," she said, ushering everyone inside. "We have lots of food, so grab a plate and help yourselves."

A nearby table was heaped with pans of baked ziti, cold cuts, and salads.

No one spoke. Smiles sagged into frowns. Sammie's face dropped with despair. She examined the fallen faces, "Don't tell me," she added.

"We already ate," Grace admitted through a sheepish grin. No one seemed to know whether to laugh or cry. There was an uneasy silence.

"I'm sorry," Esther added. "I didn't know. I wasn't sure."

Suddenly, Stevie appeared beside Sammie. "Esther!" he exclaimed.

"Stevie," Esther answered mournfully. "I'm *so* sorry, I didn't know, you were—"

"Pinch me! Tell me I'm dreaming," Stevie marveled, interrupting her in mid-sentence. "I figured the next time I'd see you was when I was dead," he added, laughing at the silliness of his own words. "And now, you're telling me you're sorry! My God, this is wonderful!"

"It's good to see you again, Stevie," Esther continued. "But, you see, you have to understand what happened—"

"There's no need to explain," Stevie interrupted again, shaking his head and dismissing her with a sweep of his fleshy hand. "I remember exactly what happened. I was there, too, you know. Apology accepted. Now, everybody come inside and sit down. Have something to eat. We have a lot of catching up to do."

"Twenty-five *years,* Stevie."

"So, you'll eat slowly."

SURVIVAL HINTS

1. Don't blame your sibling(s) if your parents don't do what you think is right with their will.
2. Always try to resolve sibling disputes before too much time goes by; if you don't, the time might come when it's too late to say you're sorry.
3. Don't wait for the other person to make the first move.
4. The sooner you reestablish contact after a rift, the easier it'll be for everyone.

The Christmas War

Sheila Myers

THE IDEA OF BRINGING a two-week-old colicky infant on an airplane full of germ-infested holiday travelers should have kept me away, but I succumbed to the relentless tugging of my mother to corral the troops for our first Christmas together since the family had experienced a series of tragedies.

We have never been the level-headed family depicted on syrupy sitcoms. Every one of us has exhibited traits of borderline personality disorder, and my mother is a classic enabler. Past reunions have left us in states of either ebullient rapture or vicious revenge. No middle ground in my family. Our get-togethers were often so turbulent that they made *National Lampoon's Christmas Vacation* look like a serious PBS documentary.

Despite our history, it still didn't occur to any of us that this holiday gathering had *disaster* written all over it in neon capital letters. We converged unwittingly after enduring long plane rides and car rides through northern Michigan back roads covered with five feet of snow (and still falling).

Eighteen months previously, a fire had destroyed my parents' home and most of its contents. To recoup their loss, Mom and Dad had to sue the insurance company and the inept agent who wrote the deficient policy. As if that wasn't enough, six months after the fire, Dad died of a heart attack.

Mom won the legal battle. When she had rebuilt her home, it was bigger and better than before. With barely enough time to sweep up the sawdust, she prepared to put her severely fractured family back together. She filled the refrigerator with food, bought a stereo, and borrowed furniture. We ate meals sitting at a patio table and slept on an eclectic collection of futons, rollaways, and blow-up mattresses. Mom's uncensored decorating whims resulted in a dizzying display of incongruous floral wallpaper patterns that probably contributed to the pandemonium of that Christmas.

The week started out pleasantly enough: humorous chats around the fireplace, friendly games of cards. Then, tempers escalated during a Monopoly game when my sister Katie was forced to declare bankruptcy because she couldn't pay the rent on Park Place with a hotel.

"You did that on purpose," Katie said to the intensely competitive Marie, who bought the hotel just before Katie rolled the dice.

"Oh, get over it. It's just a game." Katie collected her money, threw it in the middle of the board, and stomped off.

After a quiet dinner one night, we collected ourselves on the living-room sectional to relax. My brother, Frank, suddenly appeared with his electric guitar and began picking out his rendition of Van Halen's "Eruption." If you're not familiar with the tune, it sounds a lot like the music of Jimi Hendrix. Not exactly after-dinner music. The rest of us looked at each other and rolled our eyes. The hypersensitive Frank caught our reaction, unplugged his guitar, and stormed out of the room.

By day four, my own version of shock and awe commenced, triggered by Mom's insistence that she stay at home with my two kids while the rest of us went cross-country skiing. This didn't sit right with Linda, the spoiled youngest child.

"Sorry I'm not popping out babies," she yelled. "That's all you seem to care about."

I grabbed my colicky infant, who was screaming mercilessly, and ran for cover upstairs where my four-year-old, nauseated from the flu, vomited into the puke bowl. On my way, I glimpsed Linda thrusting her middle finger at Kate, who was struggling to maneuver a pair of skis out the door.

For the next two days, we hurled insults and accusations as if they were Scud missiles.

"You can't even hold a job for more than a year."

"You think you're perfect just because you're married and have two kids."

"How come nobody ever listens to me?"

We found ourselves ambushed by the intense emotions that invaded the house and took no prisoners—emotions that had festered for months: jealousy, anger, grief, and revenge, offset by an occasional burst of joy. We were desperately trying to blame our misery on each other, as if that would make it all go away. But the responsibility for those unfortunate events lay with no one. Outside, the snow fell peacefully from a steel gray sky and the mercury hovered at zero. On Christmas Day, we gathered around the tree to open our presents and barely had the energy to show our enthusiasm over a book light or a CD, but my mother mustered up the "oohs" and "ahs," her incessant Pollyanna-ish attitude a sharp contrast to our somber expressions.

In the waning hours of another memorable family gathering, my mother turned into a dutiful army nurse, tending our wounds and soothing us with bowls of turkey soup and slices of Buche de Noel. We headed home looking like shell-shocked soldiers slapped back into reality by a brutal superior officer.

Thankfully, time is a salve to the wounded bonds of family. The tattered fibers of that bond have healed and are now stronger than before. Subsequent reunions have erupted in more skirmishes. I often ask myself why I continue to participate in these gatherings, but in my heart I know the answer. Despite the potential for explosive interaction, I love those guys. We are like prisoners of war, bound together by genes and a shared history. That's the beauty of families, even dysfunctional ones.

SURVIVAL HINTS

1. If you know there will be skirmishes ahead, try not to fixate on little things.
2. Live and let live; try to focus on the positives.
3. Ignore as much as you can without bursting a blood vessel.

4

When Holidays Are Horrid

Aunt Blanche's Hair
Pamela K. Brodowsky

Uncle Reggie's Thanksgiving
Alonzo Gross

Aunt Reba and Her Christmas Clones
Madison Moore

The Turkey in the Room
Christina Michael

Now Hear This!
Toni Scott

Festive Foul-Up
John Tomaino

The food, the friends, the good cheer equals the holidays. The family plus the holidays equals the screaming, the fighting, the endless carrying on about absolutely nothing, the getting in the way, the unwanted help, and the lame advice. What are you to do if you're going to survive until the New Year?

Take the following quiz to see how skilled you are at handling holiday minefields when the family gathers.

Sanity Quiz

This year you are the lucky one—you get to plan and host the main holiday event, and all the relatives are coming—the whole clan. Now it's only a day away, and you are still not sure how many of them there will actually show up. But just then your phone rings—it's Aunt Susie, and she is bringing all ten of her children. They range in age from just born to twenty. You have no room for these unwanted extra guests, especially on such short notice.

Do you

A. tell her there is no way you can fit them all in your house
B. just suck it up and handle it
C. lie and tell her you've canceled the party
D. imitate a high-end restaurant and tell her she didn't reserve early enough
E. all of the above

No matter which answer you picked, you can see you're in for trouble. Could be worse, it could be a fancy wedding in an expensive hotel—then you'd really be up the creek.

Despite all the hissing and spitting, there is usually a way out that helps for everyone, keeps the peace as far as possible, and still allows the family to gather and enjoy the holiday without histrionics. That is, unless there's a runaway wig . . . but I don't want to spoil the surprises ahead, so read on.

Aunt Blanche's Hair

Pamela K. Brodowsky

GOT FAMILY? YEAH, me too, and a large one at that. You know that one family member who always sticks out more than the rest? Well, for me it was my Aunt Blanche. She had her competitors, but she took the cake.

You see, Aunt Blanche had hair. And by that I mean big hair, short hair, long hair, red hair, blonde hair, brown hair, and oh, there was also that lavender-tinted do. There was the one that looked like a crow's nest, a trap in which a misguided bird might truly have met his demise. Then there was the ole beehive, which, if I remember correctly, was the color of a brand-new shiny copper penny. All wigs!

This woman truly had the world's largest collection of the ugliest wigs I have ever seen. But to her, they weren't wigs; the various hairdos were all her own hair and, to this very day, I think she would have sworn to that on a Bible. The Bible of wig-wearers, that is.

I remember as a child gathering for the typical "all in the family" weekend get together. I hid with my cousins, giggling as the adults sat perched around the table. It was always a surprise to see the attention-getting hairdo that Aunt Blanche sported for the current festivities. Although there were many so-called get-togethers, one still sticks out in my mind, even today.

You see, in addition to being big in the hair department, Aunt Blanche weighed in at about three hundred pounds. She was loud: loud verbally and loud in her choice of clothes. I thought that maybe she was colorblind and couldn't hear. But I was wrong.

She was also one of those touchy-feely types. You know the kind: the smothering, cheek-pinching, hugging-so-tightly-that-you-can't-breathe type.

On the now-historic Sunday in question, Aunt Blanche had taken to being her usual annoying self when she decided to rub my head. And I mean repeatedly. Every minute or two would not be an exaggeration.

And being the patient soul I am, I looked to my mother for guidance.

But all I received in return was a shrug of her shoulders and a just-deal-with-it-honey nod. And any other child probably would have done just that. But I wasn't any other child. I was a go-getter. A true believer in the philosophy that if you want something done, or in this situation, not done, you have to handle the job yourself. So that is exactly what I did. At the ripe age of nine, you can take only so much guff.

My initial thoughts were to stay just out of her reach. If she couldn't reach me, she couldn't treat my head as if she were shining an apple. My original plan worked well for a while, until she got up to refill her cake plate for what I think was the third time.

She just couldn't resist touching my head—it was like a magnet and she was a gargantuan piece of metal. Cake plate in hand, the woman with the big hair gave my head its last rubbing.

I think at that very moment the blood in my body reached its boiling point. I clearly remember the "Oh, please don't" look on my mother's face as my arm extended up to the massive woman's hair. I tore into her wig like a nine-year-old digging through the grass looking for a bunny in her Easter basket. I messed that woman's hair until I felt I had inflicted the equal amount of annoyance due her.

What I didn't immediately realize was that during the process of this hair-messing event, I had turned her wig around. Her bangs were now over her ear instead of her eyes. I had revealed the age-old family secret of the origin of Blanche's hair. I had put an end to a decade-long betting extravaganza.

I didn't hear much more about the incident except "You shouldn't have done that"—followed by a giggle or two from the front seat of my parents' Cadillac on the ride home. And that could have been because I had done something they had wanted to do for a very long time. Or maybe it was because my father came home with the wig-pool money.

To this day, my head remains my own and only for touching by the person of my choice.

SURVIVAL HINTS

1. Take control of what you need to control to save your own sanity.
2. Never let petty annoyances fester.
3. Sometimes it's better to act out rather than speak out.
4. And always remember: Even if they are ugly, they are still your family!

Uncle Reggie's Thanksgiving

Alonzo Gross

EVER SINCE I CAN REMEMBER, "Uncle" Reggie was always a fixture at our family functions and events. Though not a blood relative, he was family nonetheless. We could always count on him to entertain and bewilder us with his eccentricities and off-the-wall philosophies.

Reginald Billy Jackson, or Uncle Reggie, was born on April 11, 1948. However, depending on whom he talked to, the year of his birth ranged from 1955 to 1959. To say that Reggie was an exaggerator of the truth is an understatement of colossal proportions.

At an early age, Uncle Reggie lost his mother in a freak car accident. His father, Reggie Sr., was placed in a mental institution after experimenting with LSD. He claimed he had fathered an extraterrestrial baby named Tulip.

Having lost both his mother and father, Uncle Reggie took up a hobby that would help him to escape his pain and alter his reality. Uncle Reggie decided to become a compulsive liar; not just any old compulsive liar, but the best the world has ever seen.

Fast forward to 1966. Uncle Reggie was eighteen years old and a high school graduate. The Vietnam War was in full swing, and Reggie was keen to enlist and do his part in defending his country. He soon discovered that the real-life military was a lot different from the portrayals he had seen on television as a child; needless to say, he was dishonorably discharged just two years later. The reason for his discharge is unknown, but sources close to the family claim that he was discharged for dressing in women's clothing and referring to himself as "Private Patricia." Unfortunately, Uncle Reggie next fell prey to drug and alcohol abuse, just as his father had. This dependency had caused him to lose numerous jobs and fail in relationships, and his compulsive lying put him into many compromising situations.

For example, there was the time he went to the local newspaper dressed in drag and said he was Michael

Jackson's estranged wife. His face was plastered on every local newspaper, and he was even featured on the 10:00 p.m. news. It was soon determined that he was lying, but not before he had gained a local following that hoped to witness his next publicity stunt. What few people knew (though perhaps the military had an inkling!) was that Uncle Reggie had a hidden talent: cross-dressing.

But Uncle Reggie was also an ingenious chef; for this reason, in addition to being a close friend of the family, he was appointed the head cook at many of our family functions.

My most memorable recollection of Uncle Reggie was my first encounter with him. It was Thanksgiving Day, 1989, and I was excited about going to Aunt Michelle's house for the holidays. She had two sons who were about my age.

I was happily playing video games with my cousins Ricky and Moody when in walks Uncle Reggie. At first, I thought he was another aunt, or perhaps an old friend of Aunt Michelle's, but when he began speaking, I realized that he was a man. My eleven-year-old mind couldn't decide whether I wanted to run or to laugh. I noticed that my cousins had half-embarrassed, half-terrified looks on their faces.

Uncle Reggie was decked out in a leather miniskirt, orange-and-green high heels, a pink blouse, full makeup, and a curly blonde wig streaked with black. In all my adolescent confusion, I did what any eleven-year-old boy would do: I began laughing hysterically.

This didn't go over well, and everyone glared at me.

Finally, it was time to sit down to Thanksgiving dinner. Aunt Michelle let us kids sit at our own table; the grownups sat at a table nearby. This was a long-standing tradition in our family.

After begging my aunt, I was allowed to sit at the grownups' table. The food was served, and it was an impressive array indeed. I was looking forward to eating, not just because the food smelled delicious, but also because I wanted a chance to see the interaction between Uncle Reggie and the rest of the family.

Everyone was waiting for Uncle Reggie to make his entrance and join us at the table. He was in the kitchen feeling extremely nervous, not because he was wearing makeup but because he thought it was smeared. Uncle Reggie was a perfectionist.

Aunt Michelle, in an attempt to break the ice, told Uncle Reggie that the turkey was delicious. Feeling confident, he decided to discuss his colorful life with the family.

He proceeded to tell the family that he was going to marry the famous rapper P. Diddy, whom he had met at Gary Coleman's birthday party. He also revealed that he had learned how to cook so well by studying under the watchful eyes of Captain Crunch and Colonel Sanders. His clothing was made by Donatella Versace herself, whom he had met through Stevie Wonder's cousin. Finally, he let everyone know that he was going to blackmail Bill Gates, the reason being that he was Bill Gates's mistress.

This was the last straw for Aunt Michelle; she stood up, ready to put Uncle Reggie in his place. Seeing what was about to happen, Uncle Reggie put his head down, partly from shame and partly from sheer terror.

He must have moved his head too quickly because off came his wig—it fell right into the beautiful turkey. There was a slight pause in the room, and then everyone began to roar with laughter—that is, everyone but Uncle Reggie.

He grabbed his wig and attempted to run out of the room, but he hadn't yet mastered the art of wearing high heels. Nor did he see Aunt Michelle's cat, Zipper, crouched directly in his way.

Uncle Reggie tripped and fell face first into the stuffing. Meanwhile, Zipper ran off with Uncle Reggie's wig. Uncle Reggie, with stuffing in his face, chased down Zipper—only to have his wig torn to shreds. Everyone was in stitches.

After cleaning himself off, Uncle Reggie revealed that he had started cross-dressing after the death of his mother. He felt that by wearing women's clothing he resembled his late mother. In doing so, he would keep her alive and in physical form. The compulsive lying was something he had started as a child in an attempt to gain acceptance.

"We love you just the way you are," said Aunt Michelle. "You don't have to do these things." This statement by Aunt Michelle caused Uncle Reggie to burst into tears. Aunt Michelle and the family surrounded Uncle Reggie and they all embraced him in a group hug.

Whether he knew it or not, he had brought the family closer together. This Thanksgiving was special because many members of the family expressed their innermost feelings. Uncle Reggie felt validated because his family loved him so much. The love radiated throughout the remainder of that day, making this Thanksgiving a huge success.

Uncle Reggie died of cancer in September 1999. We will remember him as a great cook and an interesting, sensitive human being.

The family was shocked to find out that Uncle Reggie had left the bulk of his money to a cancer research fund.

I think about him every time I see a well-dressed African American woman. In a moment of clarity, epiphany, and infinite wisdom, he told me, and I quote, "Never play leap frog with a unicorn."

SURVIVAL HINTS

1. Before you judge a family member, get to know that person because you might learn something.
2. Say what you mean but don't be mean when you say it.
3. Never argue with fools because from a distance people can't tell who is the fool.
4. Use patience as a means to arrive at the truth.
5. Empathy is the key: Remember we are all human beings.
6. All you have is your family and all they have is you.
7. Don't wait until it's too late to tell a family member that you love him or her.

Aunt Reba and Her Christmas Clones

Madison Moore

EVERY YEAR, FOR AS many as I can remember, my entire family has gathered to celebrate the richness of the holiday season. The foods and their aromas alone could feed a lifetime of memories.

The scent of turkey wafting through the air at the break of dawn and the sweetness of cookies, candies, and pies were all just part of the scene. Sharing a glass of eggnog with a long-lost cousin, listening intently to Nat King Cole wail out a Christmas tune, watching my mother frantically prepare enough food to feed a small army—it was all delightful, an event worth waiting for, wishing for, and anticipating.

At least, it was until now.

My mother had hosted this gala event for thirty years, so I decided it was time to relieve her of her duties and give her a chance to sit back and enjoy it as we had for so many years. And I wanted to give my own children a chance to celebrate it as I had: a joyous time at home, a holiday filled with magic and happiness.

Little did I know that this was the year my long lost Aunt Reba and her family were planning to reintroduce themselves into our lives after a long and desirable, dare I say enjoyable, separation.

Aunt Reba was a first-class troublemaker. She could fudge up a one-car funeral with her meddlesome ways. She was loud and boisterous, big and ugly, and she had a natural knack for bringing up topics that were sure to stir the family kettle. Her children, one boy, one girl, could have been her clones. They couldn't be any more her spitting image if she had infused them with her own genes by injecting them directly and without help from her husband.

Back to the story. I remember that fateful day as if it were yesterday. I was in the kitchen—it was December 23, just two days before my first whole-family dinner. The children and I were busy making Christmas cookies—pinwheels, peanut butter kisses, and gingerbread men with little raisin eyes. My husband, Sam, walked into the room as eagerly as if he had found some forgotten treasure and said, "Honey, there is someone on the phone, she says she's your Aunt Reba."

I dropped my cookie tin and stood paralyzed. My children and husband were staring at me intently, wondering whether I had suffered a stroke. I was frozen in place. I couldn't move. All I could think was, "No, way, not me. This can't be happening."

Time stood still until Sam asked, "You have an Aunt Reba? Why didn't you ever tell me about her?" I had never told him about her because I didn't want to remember she had ever existed. Not to mention that on the occasions I had seen her, I was embarrassed: not for me, but for her. "We'll talk about that later," I replied. I couldn't begin to fathom explaining this with the children in the room.

"Are you going to answer the phone?" Sam shot back.

The walk down the hall was what I imagine the walk to the gas chamber on death row would be like. All I could think about was that my Christmas dinner party, into which I had put so much energy and planning, was about to be destroyed.

Then it came to me: Maybe she just needed a phone number, an address, or something along those lines. I stood next to the phone for what felt like an eternity before getting up enough nerve to reach for the receiver. My voice crackled as I answered with the feeble hello of a mouse. That was the last word I said until I replaced the receiver into its cradle. You didn't get to talk with Aunt Reba—you just listened. There was no way to insert a word into any conversation when she was a participant.

After sliding down the wall I was leaning on to keep myself from fainting, the little wicker-back caught me as I slid into a sitting position.

Sam had kept one eye planted on me since I had picked up the phone. Slowly he moved down the long hall, almost as if he were tip-toeing on a surface of eggshells. Knowing full well by my initial reaction that I might lose it at any moment, he gently asked, "Is everything alright, honey? Are you okay?"

I don't remember what I said to him because it all spewed out of me as if a volcano were erupting. There was crying, anger, and a whole bunch of jumbled words and mumblings. There were words I had never used before, words that didn't even belong together, words that I now thank God my children weren't in the room to hear.

She was coming and she was bringing *them.* "Oh, my God, what am I going to do?" was all I could say.

Sam, the kind and light-hearted soul that he is, replied, "But she can't be *that* bad."

"How did she get our number?" I gasped. "How did she find us?" Mother, my mother—her sister—must have been Reba's first call. I pressed the speed dial button for Mom. And sure enough, she confirmed my suspicions.

Aunt Reba had called her first, and my mother being the sweet little woman she was didn't know what else to do but send her my way. Mom thought that as a protective reflex I would instantly find the wits to ward her off. Only I never had the chance. Because I couldn't speak. Because I wasn't prepared. Because you need warning before a bomb like this is dropped on your head; you need time to plan your defensive strategy before going to the battle front.

Now my only recourse was to develop a foolproof containment plan so that, no matter what, this woman could not ruin the first of what I hoped would be many holiday dinners at my house.

That night, after the children went to bed, Sam and I spent the evening finalizing the details of the upcoming party. I wanted everything to be perfect. From the table settings to the centerpieces to the decorations and food, everything was to be done in a certain special way.

I sat at the kitchen table thumbing through a Martha Stewart *Living Christmas* edition when I saw it.

Here was the answer I needed—the solution to the Aunt Reba problem.

"I know how I can keep her quiet. I've got it," I shrieked to Sam, my smile as big as Santa's. Sam looked up from his cup of hot cocoa. "You're still worried about that?" he asked.

"Place cards," I shouted. There was not enough room for her and hers at the main table, which was already full to capacity, the seating elbow-to-elbow.

"We need to bring in the card table from the garage," I cackled. That was it, thank you, Martha!

Sam and I placed the card table far enough from the main table so that Lady Loudmouth would be unable to speak with the other guests while dinner was being served, at least not without a megaphone.

I had already begun crafting Martha's place cards when Sam turned to me with a twinkle in his eye: "I knew you would find a way to get that Christmas spirit back!" he said. All I could do was smile at his sweet but mischievous comment.

Christmas Day came and went, and so did Aunt Reba and her two clones. The table-for-three plan worked perfectly. There were no bad memories, only new, fond ones of our first and now annual Christmas gatherings, and the small and insignificant memory of a very large woman in a leopard print jumper was far in the background.

Christmas was saved forever!

SURVIVAL HINTS

1. When in desperate need of some crafty solutions for your entertaining dilemmas, don't forget Martha Stewart.
2. Be prepared for the worst, because it makes the best look all that much better.
3. Remember that shrewdness comes with practice.
4. Just grin and bear it—it's only one day.

The Turkey in the Room

Christina Michael

FOR THANKSGIVING ONE YEAR AGO, my husband and his immediate family decided we should all stay in the Catskills together. My in-laws have a newly renovated house and wanted us there for the four days.

Now that my husband, Chuck, was married with his own children, it was something he'd dreamed of doing. He had visions of the family sitting together, thoroughly enjoying each other's company. I had visions of slitting my wrists.

I used any argument I could think of to go visit my family instead, and even used the argument that I wasn't going to see them for Christmas, either. I tried to get him to stay home Wednesday evening and travel on Thanksgiving morning, and even suggested we come home Saturday morning; but being a trooper, and a sucker for punishment, he wanted the joyous family holiday (torture) to begin as soon as possible and to last for as long as possible.

So up we went—one husband bent on reliving every childhood dream he could remember, a reluctant wife, one five-year-old boy, one seven-year-old boy, one cat, and one beagle.

We would be joining the domineering, opinionated, judgmental group of one mother-in-law, one father-in-law, two uncles and their spouses, one aunt, one sister-in-law, and one brother-in-law (who can top the rest of the family with his domineering, opinionated, and judgmental pronouncements).

We did enjoy the first evening and the holiday, even though one aunt was afraid of cats and the dog bounded unceremoniously around his newly discovered "friends." When things became too chaotic during those four days, I'd go upstairs, shut our bedroom door, and read. As long as Chuck was entertaining the kids, or they were entertaining themselves, I knew I was in the clear for a little while.

On Friday, the aunts and uncles went home, leaving the in-laws and Chuck's sister and her husband. It was raining and I wanted to go around the antique shops with Chuck to get out of the house and away from the remaining crowd, but the sister and her husband wanted to come. Of course, Chuck gladly included them while I smiled through gritted teeth. My in-laws had agreed to watch our menagerie and I was looking for alone time with my beloved—but he wasn't thinking of cuddling under the umbrella, holding hands, sipping a hot drink while looking at antiques. It was the more the merrier for Chuck!

How did I deal with this development? Having one umbrella per couple helped because you can't get close to another couple that is also under an umbrella. Umbrellas make wonderful "personal space" savers. Also, as we walked from store to store, we would inevitably become separated. When Chuck asked where they were, I'd tell him and then suggest that we move on to the next store: "They'll catch up," I would reassure him. They always did catch up, but not for long enough to interfere with my relaxation.

By the time we arrived home for dinner, I felt better, but I knew that two more days were going to grate on my nerves. The brother-in-law has a habit of riling up my kids to the point that they are screaming and tackling him while the rest of us are trying to talk. Then he tells them to stop as if they were robots equipped with an "off" switch. Thankfully—and a little surprisingly, I must add—my husband actually told the darling brother-in-law to stop making the kids go nuts, which helped.

Then, of course, the dog's being underfoot was an issue for my sister-in-law. By Friday night, she was yelling at him to leave her alone. Fortunately, he was able to spend lots of time outside in the large yard enjoying the fall weather.

On Saturday morning, I told Chuck that only the four of us, meaning us and our two kids (yes, I had to say this *specifically*) were going to do something together for the entire day. So we decided to hike in the woods with our dog in the morning, come back to the house at lunch time, and then take off in the car for the afternoon.

When the kids were not within earshot, we rehashed specific events to vent our feelings. I expect that everyone back at the house was doing the same about us. Then I told Chuck in no uncertain terms that we were going home after breakfast on Sunday morning because I'd had enough. He actually agreed.

So we survived. Between intermittently hiding and reading in my bedroom, umbrellas and separate stores in the rain, the husband finally speaking up, hiking in the woods, venting to my significant other, and finally being specific about my needs, we made it through four whole days of in-law holiday fun.

Next year, we're visiting *my* family.

SURVIVAL HINTS

1. Plan some activities alone or with your immediate family to take a break from the crowd.
2. Be polite if you have to assert yourself.
3. Be sure your car holds only the number of people you want to take everywhere.
4. Try to limit the amount of time you'll have to stay.
5. Pack an umbrella, just in case!

Now Hear This!

Toni Scott

"WHAT? DID YOU SAY SOMETHING? I didn't hear you!" Uncle Jack would say in reply to just about anything, even when he was the one who asked you the question himself. "Eh?"

You see, Uncle Jack wasn't hard of hearing, he just had selective hearing. You know the kind—men who hear only what they want to hear, and nothing else. The kind who can tune out a bull stampede through the middle of the living room but not only can hear, but recite, word for word, some dumb low-budget movie. That's right, the men in your life aren't the only ones; we all have them. They come by the bunch, kind of like bananas.

One Thanksgiving, we were blessed with five of these bananas: They were all together in one room, perched as usual in front of a television, watching football and carrying on like a bunch of fools. "Go, Go, Go!" they screamed as their favorite players ran around the field. Every time one of their favorites scored a touchdown, they jumped up and down as if they had a nest full of bees buzzing around in their jeans.

Meanwhile, the kitchen was buzzing, too, but with women preparing the holiday feast and shaking off the loud noises coming from those overripe bananas in the living room.

Normally, food call is one of the few times you can get a man's full attention. Well, of course, there is sex, too. If you yelled "Time for sex!" at the top of your lungs, you would probably get at least a stir out of them. But when they're watching football on Thanksgiving Day, even sex may not do it—never mind the feedbag. It might normally do the trick, just not on this day.

Anyhow, the food was ready and presented beautifully on the table. As the rest of us sat down, one of the women, the wife of one of the bananas, called from the kitchen: "Time to eat!"

Waiting for the men to arrive before beginning to eat usually takes about a nanosecond. But not this time. We waited and waited for about ten minutes. Finally, Wife Number Two belted out to her banana, "Dinner's ready!"—but still no men.

There we sat, the once-hot beautiful dinner that we'd spent hours preparing now growing cold. Then one of the more mischievous wives said, "Let's eat without them." The vote was unanimous.

So we did just that. We ate, cleaned up, put the left-overs in the refrigerator, poured ourselves some coffee, and sat back down to relax.

Just then, Uncle Jack strolled through the dining room on his way to the bathroom. Noticing that we were eating our after-dinner pie, he bellowed, "How long till dinner?"

"Now hear this," replied Aunt Sally. "It'll be ready as soon as you and the other bananas in the living room get up and heat yourselves up some."

After a bit of grumbling on the part of the disgruntled men, they finally ate their warmed-over turkey. Served them right, and served by themselves!

SURVIVAL HINTS

1. If your man is selectively hard of hearing, retrain him by speaking in a whisper.

2. If he's late to the table, feel free to eat without him.
3. If he says "What?" more than once a day, he is a banana.
4. Believe it or not, bananas like him can take care of themselves. Stop waiting on him and rest up!

Festive Foul-Up

John Tomaino

"I DON'T WANT OTHER people crapping in my toilet."

That was my father's initial response upon hearing that our family would be hosting this year's Christmas dinner.

Upon reflection, I think he probably made a lot of sense. Around twenty of Mum's relatives—all despised by my father in remarkably equal proportions—would certainly struggle to control their bowels. Especially after a hearty Christmas dinner.

But no good sense could intervene. Christmas Day arrived and the doorbell rang like a continuous two-tone samba. Dad greeted each relative at the door with varying levels of enthusiasm, carefully guided by the knowledge of what gifts they had bestowed the year before. No. His memory was not *that* good; he kept a record. A page with a list of names in one column and the approximate value of the gifts in the other.

My father hasn't seen the inside of a shopping center for years, but seemed to have an uncanny ability to estimate the value of the disparate gifts: silverware, diamond earings, electric toothbrushes. They all received a dollar value. And if he was in doubt, he erred on the side of caution: a wise strategy in these uncertain times.

Our relatives graciously accepted his gifts in return, all purchased within strict tolerances of the approximate value of the gifts that he had received. If they were disappointed by the quality of his gifts, they only had themselves to blame.

Nobody dared complain about Dad; he took criticism as well as he took an interest in the lives of Mum's family, which is to say, not well. But there was always one. One relative who didn't heed the warning. Who ventured too far. The pockets of conversations hushed as Auntie Rina went where no relative had gone before: beyond the small-talk.

"We didn't think you'd make it, Tony," she said.

Mum never knew whether to set the table for Dad; he hated making plans, being tied to an appointment, or having people know his movements. He'd always say that he might be working, even for the Christmas dinner. Apparently, lots of people are interested in sheet metal work on Christmas Day. Go figure.

"You can say that again," he replied.

What the hell does *that* mean? It was what everyone was thinking. There was a hidden message in his reply. Of that they were certain. But what did he *really* mean? Dad spoke only in cryptic messages. How I wished he could make his point with invisible ink; at least we could hold it to a fluorescent light. But we had to rely on the accumulated wisdom of the Tomaino family, whose members concluded that he must have been pissed about something.

At about this time Mum awkwardly shoves a plate of food in between them. Food is the perfect sedative for an Italian family. And it's hard to argue when your mouth is filled with a succulent cheese-filled meatball. My family's manic preoccupation with food always surprises me. Sure, it *should* be a preoccupation for every family; they can't live without it. But it's still a basic human function. Nobody gets excited about *breathing,* do they? Yet try eating Mum's lasagna if you have a collapsed lung.

I wish I could say that Dad's a changed man. That I now enjoy our Christmas dinners. That important lessons have been learned and can now be shared. As a man who didn't care much about mathematics once said: Two out of three ain't bad.

I *do* enjoy my Christmas dinners. And I *do* have an important message for others. But no. He's *not* a changed man. Each tray of Mum's lasagna is different. And no two Christmas's are quite the same. So there *must* be hope. And that's what gets me through the experience. (That, and a nice cool bottle of antacid).

For those facing an unpopular relative at Christmas get-togethers, here are my top three survival tips.

SURVIVAL HINTS

1. The partners of problem relatives are the ones who suffer most. Concentrate on supporting them because they also have the best chance of curbing the obnoxious behavior of their partners.
2. Keep conversations brief. Remember that even the largest telecommunication companies promote *Short Message Services*.
3. Turkey skin contains the natural sedative L-tryptophan. So when it all gets too much, knock yourself out and eat it all!

5

When Food Is the Issue

The Snail Invasion
Evelyn M. Fazio

You Can Dress Them Up . . .
Bethany Gould

The Uninvited Guest
Alexis Rizzuto

The Food-Poisoning Neighbors
Ginny Chandoha

Immodium Blues
Susan Berlin

The Revenge of the Chocoholics
Evelyn M. Fazio

We, the people, love to eat. And if you didn't feed your guests, just imagine how much shorter their visits would be. Hmm. Now there's some food for thought. To check your skill at handling your guests' food issues, take the following quiz:

Sanity Quiz

You are having dinner for a few friends and family members. Not a big get-together, just a small, intimate group. Five of your six guests love your lasagna, which just happens to take you all day to prepare because you insist upon making everything from scratch.

Your sixth guest, although she eats your lasagna, and plenty of it, consistently complains of your choice of food. She's on a diet, she can't eat gluten, she's doing no carbs, she's lactose intolerant. Pick one!

Do you

A. warn her ahead of time so that she can bring her own entrée

B. make her a separate dish on top of all your other preparations

C. tell her that maybe next time you'll make something she likes

No matter which answer you selected, you obviously need to be prepared for all kinds of eventualities when entertaining guests at your home dinner table. There are gems of wisdom ahead, whether it's feeding—and poisoning—the neighborhood, handling escaped entrées, suffering the consequences of too much cappuccino, dealing with health-food nuts, or rationing your chocolate reserves. So read on for the best laughs and sound advice from those of us who've already been there and survived!

The Snail Invasion

Evelyn M. Fazio

WHEN I WAS ELEVEN YEARS OLD, my mother and I went to Florida to visit my grandparents. My father, who had his own construction company, was too busy to go with us, so he stayed at home to work and guard the nest. Being Italian, my grandmother, Dad's mother Angelina, decided to move in to "take care of him" while we were gone.

Off we went to Florida. And Dad and Grandma went directly to the kitchen. Remember, we're Italian! They began whipping up all sorts of Sicilian delicacies that neither Mom nor I would ever even look at, from stews made from beef and pork organs, which I still shudder to think about, to various squishy seafood dishes such as scungille (conch) and similar delights.

As I imagine it, the cooking provided them a great time together and the snail-fest would have been the highlight. A good time was had by all, both in Florida and in New Jersey.

When Mom and I returned home after several weeks in the Florida sun, all seemed well. We were happy to be home, Dad was glad to see us, and Grandma was glad to return to her own house. Things were just great, that is, until Mom ventured back into her big yellow kitchen. We heard a muffled shriek.

Her formerly pristine kitchen was now a festival of grease, fingerprints, and stains, and that was only the cabinets and countertops. I can't even describe the state of the floor, and even the ceiling had a few spots that we didn't want to know about.

After a solid week of scrubbing, the kitchen was returned to its former sparkling condition. All was well; that is, until Mom decided to make a pot of pasta sauce. Another muffled shriek.

Inside the cabinet where the pots and pans were housed, there was a veritable army of dried-up snails. They had obviously made their escape when being soaked in water before being cooked. Grandma and Dad must have forgotten to put a lid on the pot in which they soaked!

There were snails everywhere. Stuck to pot lids, pot handles, pan bottoms, the insides of the cabinets, anywhere you looked—snails. As I contemplated the legions of snails that had made their way into the cabinets, I had to wonder how many, if any, Dad and Grandma had actually eaten. Either they had bought a triple batch or they had eaten only two apiece.

When confronted with the remains of the snail fugitives, my father shrugged his shoulders and filled us in:

"We were soaking the snails overnight, and when we came into the kitchen in the morning, Grandma nearly fell over from shock. They were everywhere! On the walls, in the sink, on the curtains, crawling up the table legs—we couldn't believe our eyes. I should have taken a picture, but we were too stunned by the sight. Then we couldn't stop laughing. We captured as many as we could find, but I guess we missed a few. It just happened the day before you got home, so I guess we didn't go into the pot cabinet again."

My mother narrowed her eyes at Dad, who beat a hasty retreat to the safety of his workshop in the basement.

About eight years later, when I was in college in Connecticut, my friends came from three states to dine at Chez Fazio; they had realized that this was the place to eat whenever possible, so there was always a steady stream of them dropping in.

One Saturday evening, about an hour before the hungry hoards were about to descend, I went into the pot cabinet to retrieve the rarely used, huge pasta pot, which could accommodate the upcoming feast of calamari in red sauce over linguini for eight.

As I reached into the far corner of the cabinet to retrieve the garbage-can-sized pot, I saw an unexpected appendage that brought back hilarious memories.

There, on the turned-upside-down pot lid, was the final remnant of Grandma and Dad's snail-fest so many years ago. Grandma had passed away a few years earlier, and I'm sure that wherever she was, she had a really good last laugh. I know that Mom, Dad, and I sure did.

SURVIVAL HINTS

1. If you invite a guest chef, don't be surprised at anything you find when you return to your status of head chef.
2. If your mother-in-law takes over your kitchen, be prepared for disaster and try to maintain your equilibrium if you want to stay married afterwards.
3. If you decide to prepare snails, make sure you put something heavy on the pot you soak them in.

You Can Dress Them Up … But You Can't Take Them Out

Bethany Gould

I HAVE ALWAYS BEEN a people person, and I delight in visits from family and friends. I love having a house full of people! I thrive on the gathering of many minds and unique experiences, the sharing of funny stories, and just the variety and differences of our daily routines. I would rather cook for ten than for two any day. Some would say I am insane. I say the more the merrier.

I have a large family, five children, but unfortunately they are all grown and living away from home.

That leaves just my husband and me in this great big hollow home where in the old days the noise level was so high that I could not even hear myself scream. But now my house is a quiet and serene place, where you can even hear a mouse breathing. So when a guest, invited or not, stops by, I am more than appreciative of the company.

Anyhow, a guest is always a guest, and all are treated as such in my home. I have one long-time friend, Betty, who moved south years ago for her job. So when Betty calls to say she is coming to visit, she means she is coming for the week. I love Betty with all my heart. She is one of the kindest souls I have ever met, truly a good person to have on your roster of friends. And she's one of the most helpful, self-sufficient guests ever to grace my doorway. Always going out of her way to make things more comfortable, help out around the house, and get things done, Betty is one of my best friends.

So when the phone rang on this particular Saturday afternoon, hearing Betty's voice on the other end was a real treat. She was in town for business and had managed to get a few extra days to spend with us. I was in sheer heaven. Not only was my best friend coming to visit me, but for the next few days I would have someone to talk to other than my husband, Frank. Don't misunderstand. I love Frank to death.

But it's really nice to have someone else, someone a little more entertaining around once in a while. You can only say so much to a husband of twenty-eight years. That is, of course, other than "What's that terrible smell—was that you?" "Get your laundry off the floor," or "Have you taken the garbage out yet?"

Jumping up and down at least on the inside (I don't know whether I'm capable of it on the outside anymore), I ran into the den where Frank was perched in the corner under his reading light. "Frank, Betty is coming." I belted out like a young child who just found out Santa was on his way. Frank just grumbled a "So what?" in his normal tone.

"I've got to get ready—she will be here in less than an hour. We have no food in the fridge. The house is a wreck, and, oh, look at my hair."

"Cut out the fuss, Bethy," he said. That was Frank's pet name for me. Well, either it was a pet name or just Frank's way of saving energy. Cutting those last three letters out of my name could tally up to a great deal of time spent over a lifetime together.

"First things first." I said. "My hair, my God." As I looked into the mirror, the reflection looking back at me was one that I was not prepared to see. I looked as if I hadn't been to the salon in months, maybe even years. Even if the house was a mess, my hair was now top priority. Betty would forgive me for the untidy house, but I would not forgive myself for the untidy me. After some much-needed primping, I was back to normal. I even had enough time to run the vacuum quickly before Betty's car swept into the drive.

Carrying on like two lunatics, Betty and I met half way up the walk. She looked wonderful, as always. I led her into the house where, by now, Frank had managed to dislodge his rear from the big leather recliner, which, by the way, was so worn that even after he stood up you could still see his imprint on the cushion. He managed to get out a quick "How are ya" before retreating upstairs to leave us to what we do best. Reminisce, laugh, and just enjoy the heck out of each other.

I made Betty a nice hot cup of coffee and we talked for hours. I got so lost in the conversation that I totally forgot that I didn't have a morsel of food in the house. It was nearing dinnertime when Frank showed his face again.

"What do you two gals expect we will be having for dinner?" he asked. "Dinner, oh my, I totally forgot," I said, putting my hands to the sides of my absent-minded head. Betty interrupted with a "Let's go out, it's my treat. I came here on short notice because I wanted to surprise you; now the least I can do is take you both to dinner."

Now if it were any other friend or family member making this offer, it would have been graciously accepted on the spot. But, you see, this was coming from Betty. And Betty's only fault that I know of is that she turned into a kind of Jekyll and Hyde in a restaurant. She was no longer the sweet, innocent, take-everything-with-a-grain-of-salt Betty. She was more like an unstable food critic who missed her doses of both Prozac and Premarin, not to mention Lithium.

It normally starts out with a general complaint to the hostess about the seating arrangement. Every time she spots a table opening up, one she would rather be seated at, we find ourselves having to pick up our belongings and move. Now the first time or two isn't all that bad, but when getting seated turns into a full-blown game of musical chairs it begins to wear on one's nerves. Not only that, but with every move you make there is one more plate or glass that has to be moved with you.

But really this is only the beginning. You have to order appetizers and Betty's is always too hot, too cold, too greasy, or just not what she ordered. Then the same thing happens when you move on to the main course: Betty's is inedible, but only after she's eaten half.

Betty gets a lot of exercise by raising her hand to attract a waiter's attention. She is the type of person who makes waiters, waitresses, and chefs spit in, stomp on, or do even worse things to your food before delivering it to your table. Trust me, I was a waitress and I know.

Frank is well aware of Betty's one bad quality. He still repeats the terrible story of Betty in restaurants to everyone he meets who hasn't already heard it, and repeatedly to me when he has nothing else to complain about. Anyway, I knew that no matter what, Frank would not be going out with us tonight just from the look on his otherwise placid face that said "You've got to be kidding!"

Now, dear Frank could have saved just himself and gotten us out of his hair, knowing full well the torture I would be going through. But instead he chose to save me. Frank donned his suit of armor, jumped on his white horse, and made the grand gesture: He offered to go pick up some take-out because he had a hankering for Chinese.

That day Frank showed me what type of man he is. Frank absolutely loves food, but he detests Chinese. When he put my sanity ahead of his hunger and personal taste, I knew I was close to his heart and not just his stomach.

Betty's short visit was otherwise uneventful. We had a great time seeing each other and, despite Betty's beastly behavior in restaurants, we will have many more wonderful times together.

SURVIVAL HINTS

1. Keep your friends close to your heart and, if necessary, home for dinner.
2. When in need of food and your sanity all at the same time, order out.
3. Never complain to the people who are preparing your meal.

The Uninvited Guest: Or, How My Brother's Pig Came to Brunch

Alexis Rizzuto

MY HUSBAND ALEX AND I had just bought our first house in October, and as the holidays approached, we wanted to have the family over to see the place. So I planned a Christmas brunch.

Mom and Dad had spent Thanksgiving in Ohio, where my brother Greg also had a new place. Our condo is in Cambridge, Massachusetts—home to Harvard and a seat of blue-state liberalism; my brother lives on a Midwestern farm, on which he raises pigs.

My parents were full of stories about the farm and eagerly passed around their stack of pictures: There's Dad in his field coat and tweed cap in the pig barn. Here he sits on a stool among the pigs, chummily sharing the morning newspaper—out loud, apparently. He quite enjoyed meeting them.

"And now I'll enjoy eating them!" he says to tease me, his staunchly vegetarian daughter. Greg had sent them back loaded with ham and bacon; they, of course, offered to bring them over for brunch and I, of course, declined.

Now, my history of trying to feed my meat-and-potatoes family is nothing but failed attempts to show them that it is possible to eat a nutritious, satisfying, and good meal without a slab of meat on your plate. As many Asian and Middle-Eastern cuisines do this much better than American, I've also tried to expand their palates. Once, after a feast of homemade falafel, hummus, tabouli, lavash bread, stuffed grape leaves, baklava, and mint tea, they concluded that the people who ate such things must be too poor to afford meat and therefore substituted these dishes.

No such mistake could be made this day. I set the table with cream-colored linens, silver, and the heirloom china; the centerpiece was an arrangement of candles and evergreens. Ella Fitzgerald sang Christmas music in the background, and the air was scented with cranberry oil. The menu: mimosas, punch, sectioned grapefruit, and blood oranges dotted with pomegranate seeds and bordered with kiwi slices in a footed glass bowl, popovers with jam, two stratas made with free-range eggs—one flavored with asparagus and cheese, the other with mushrooms and crumbled vegetarian breakfast sausage—and pound cake with hazelnut wafers to accompany the fair-trade coffee.

My family assembled at the table: Mom and Dad, Grammy, my sister, Karen, my brother, Pete, and his wife, Holly, and Alex and me. The bejeweled fruit salad was eaten without incident (though Holly had never seen pomegranates and wasn't sure she liked them); the popovers came out of the oven at just the right time; and the hearty slices of strata were served. Dad looked at the empty space on his plate and said, "You know what would make this even better? Some bacon."

"Dad, you know how I feel about meat; I don't care how well those pigs were treated."

"Don't worry," said he, "you don't have to cook it—it's all ready." And he went to the porch where he had stashed a platter of his erstwhile friends, popped it in the microwave, and proceeded to serve out heaps of bacon to anyone who wanted it. Everyone but me.

Greg had sent a salty, smoky, savory message from the heartland, and I have to admit, it smelled damned good.

SURVIVAL HINTS

1. If your guests have a preference for meat or vegetarian food, try to accommodate them as far as possible.
2. Sometimes it's best to go with the flow when your guests bring their own food.
3. It's okay to enjoy the aroma of something you don't wish to eat!

The Food-Poisoning Neighbors

Ginny Chandoha

AFTER SEVERAL YEARS OF BEGGING, my brother and his family finally came for a weekend visit. At the time, we lived in a three-bedroom, one-bathroom house.

On this particular weekend, our neighbors, who are from Sicily, were throwing a high school graduation party for their eldest son. Maria wanted everything to be perfect, and fresh, and she spent days making her own wonderful pasta and preparing the Italian dishes. All the family's friends and relatives gathered for this informal, homey event, held at the local church, on what turned out to be the hottest day of the summer. The food was delicious, and we soon gobbled up the trays of lasagna, ravioli, and stuffed shells, all of which were abundantly refilled on the buffet table. It was a glorious event, one filled with good people, good talk, good jokes, good food.

Several hours later, after we'd returned home and gone to bed, I developed a stomach ache and got up to use the bathroom. I thought it was odd that the toilet seat felt warm. No sooner had I gone back to bed than my husband was up with gastrointestinal pain of his own. We were both back in bed, our stomachs gyrating, when we heard the guest bedroom door open, the shuffle of feet down the hall, the flush of the toilet, the shuffle of feet back to the bedroom. Then, to our surprise, there was another shuffle of feet to the bathroom, then another, and another! The bathroom door had become a revolving one. When our own intestinal demands returned, we had to wait until there was a gap in the shuffle of feet; then we'd make a mad dash to the bathroom before anyone else could get there. When we opened the door, there'd be someone waiting in the hallway. After a while, the five of us just lined up in the hallway and waited our repetitive turns.

By morning, none of us, except my nephew, had gotten any sleep, and we'd each lost about five pounds from dehydration. I lamely claimed it was one way to lose weight. We interrogated my nephew and demanded to know what he'd eaten at the party, because he wasn't affected at all. We all compared our choices, some the same, some not. So why wasn't my nephew ill? He'd eaten salad, nothing else.

As soon as we concluded that we were suffering food poisoning, the phone rang. It was our neighbor, Maria. "Are you as sick as we are?" she asked with embarrassment. She advised us to go to the hospital, and once there, we were reunited with all of the other party guests. But by then, the poisoning bacteria had, for the most part, passed out of our systems, and all we wanted and needed were liquids to reconstitute ourselves.

Representatives from the Board of Health visited our neighbor's house because so many of the party-goers had ended up at the hospital. They determined that our neighbor's refrigerator hadn't kept the pre-made food at the proper temperature, and the hot summer sun hadn't helped, either.

To this day, we all laugh when we reminisce about that episode nearly twenty years ago. But what I remember most is how tender and wonderful that freshly-made pasta was. I've recently asked Maria to teach me how to make pasta. But I'll be sure to check the temperature of her refrigerator.

SURVIVAL HINTS

1. If you go to any summer outdoor food-fests, avoid creamy or mayonnaise dishes, including salads.
2. If you throw an outdoor summer party, keep the creamy and mayonnaise foods on ice.
3. Try to keep all the food in the shade.
4. Be sure not to poison your guests!

Immodium Blues

Susan Berlin

IT WAS LATE SUNDAY AFTERNOON, the end of a typical Sunday visit with the family. My parents, my sister and her family, and my family had all gathered to eat (of course) and socialize.

My mother, who loves gadgets but is phobic about their workings, had presented my sister and me with cappuccino makers—not just any old cappuccino makers but high-end, state-of-the-art cappuccino makers!

"Here you go, you both like to entertain, use them!" she commanded, for that is how my mother makes a gift. She is extremely generous, but apparently yelling is required when giving. So we made that cappuccino, and had a ball doing it. We brewed that espresso, steamed that milk, and drank and drank that coffee. We gave no thought to the stomach and bowel issues that *everyone* in my family suffers. The cappuccino tasted good, and we were having fun playing with our new toys.

When my parents went home in the late afternoon, my sister and I still had all that cappuccino to drink. Relieved, as always, when the older generation had left, we chatted for about an hour longer. Finally, my sister and her family said their goodbyes, and I continued to clean up after they had gone.

About ten minutes later, the doorbell rang. It was my sister.

Without any explanation, she pushed her way in and practically sprinted for the bathroom. Shortly thereafter, she emerged, and, grinning, she said, "That cappuccino, I knew I wouldn't make it all the way home! Do you have anything I can take for this?" I gave her the maximum dose of Immodium.

She grabbed them eagerly and swallowed them whole, with no water! I was impressed with that act and told her so. We were able to visit a little longer while the medication took its desired affect. And then, once again, the family was on its way.

Four days later, my phone rang—no hello, no salutation. It was my sister.

"I haven't gone to the bathroom in four days. When does this stuff ever wear off?" I just laughed and laughed. I recommended that she make some more cappuccino!

SURVIVAL HINTS

1. Become intimately familiar with Immodium, a modern-day medical miracle—it's binding!
2. Don't overdo the cappuccino—it's not binding!

The Revenge of the Chocoholics

Evelyn M. Fazio

WHEN I WAS A LITTLE KID, my house was full of relatives. I was an only child, but you'd never know it because I have thirty-three first cousins, and most of them were floating around the house during most of my childhood. It was great, lots of fun, and they were all nice kids, but some of them were like locusts with their appetite for candy.

Candy was a somewhat sore subject in our house. Mom, who did most of the food shopping, liked icky things like those jellied fruit slices covered in sugar, along with sour balls and other obnoxiously sweet hard candy. But my father and I preferred chocolate. Any kind, especially Hershey bars with almonds as well as Chunkys, Almond Joys, and Raisinets.

Unfortunately, Mom seemed to buy only a small amount of our preferred goodies, and the purchase always seemed to coincide with an invasion of cousins; they always devoured every scrap before we had the chance to snatch a solitary piece of the glorious confections.

One day, after one of these chocolate-depleting visits, Dad threw a fit. "Ev, do you have to always put all the good candy out when the kids come to visit? We didn't even get a chance to have one piece each!" he complained. "And now, all that's left are these awful sugared fruit slices that we don't like." Then he said to me the fateful words: "C'mon, Evie," he coaxed. "We're going candy shopping, and we're only getting what *we* like, and we're going to hide it where nobody can get it but us!"

Off we went to the candy store not far from home. This was a wonderful old store run by a wonderful gentleman named Mr. Wolf. He was probably only in his sixties at the time, but when you're only about seven, that's ancient. Mr. Wolf 's shop was part soda fountain (a place where you got ice cream sundaes, cones, and wonderful drinks such as egg creams—which contain neither!), part magazine store, and part candy emporium. In short, for a child, this was paradise.

Dad and I picked out a veritable mountain of chocolates. Everything we liked, some things we'd never tried, and all sorts of chocolates in between. We came out with a huge brown bag of goodies, both of us grinning from ear to ear. When we got into Dad's truck, we broke into the stash, unwrapping, chewing, and laughing the whole time.

On the short drive back, my father said, "We have to find a good hiding place for this stash. Otherwise your mother will put it all into the candy dishes and your cousins will vacuum it all up before we even see it, let alone eat it. What are we going to do with it all? Hmm."

"How about your workshop, Dad?" I suggested. "You have a million drawers down there in your cabinets. Even if she started looking, it'll take her a year to find it, and we should be safe for a while at least. Besides, she never really goes in there except to bring you something to drink once in a while."

"Good idea, Chip," he said. Chip was my nickname. Chip off the old block, I guess. It was his way of acknowledging that in many ways I was like him, including my choco-holism.

So down into the basement we went, with Mom calling behind us, "Where are you going? What's in the bag?"

"None of your business," he said, laughing all the way down the stairs with me right beside him.

Down in the workshop, we pondered the array of drawers and settled on one. In went the stash, except for the remaining pieces that we were still enjoying. We sat in the rec room chuckling over our Chunkys and Almond Joys, and thought of my uncle's five kids having to eat only jellied orange slices and sugared mint leaves. Served them right for being human vacuum cleaners!

Next time we had company, Mom put out the leaves and slices, along with the two or three pieces of chocolate left from the last invasion. My father and I simply smiled; we knew that after everyone went home and the dust settled, we'd be in chocolate bliss, down in the workshop, with no competition!

SURVIVAL HINTS

1. When confronted with invading guests who eat all your treats, be sure to keep a stash for yourself.
2. If someone in your life is overly generous, be glad that person isn't a miser, and be thankful that you can afford to be magnanimous.
3. Make sure you tell no one where you hide the stash!

6

When They Bring Their Kids and Pets

Why is it that other people tend to let their kids run loose like a herd of cattle in an open pasture when they are anywhere else but in their own homes? It happens all the time, from supermarkets to churches, parking lots to department stores. And when they bring them to your house, look out! From uprooted plants to traumatized pets, sometimes it's difficult to survive when kids are visited upon us! And forget about trying to feed them! Of course, our own kids, I'm sure we can all agree, are perfect!

Take the following quiz to see how well you're equipped to handle the kids who show up at your door:

Sanity Quiz

Your cousin has come to visit and she has brought all three of her children with her. You haven't seen them in a year and you are amazed by how much they have grown. And you're even more amazed by how badly they are behaving. After about an hour of watching them ransack your home without intervention from their mother, what do you do?

Do you

A. politely ask your cousin to control her kids
B. yell at them yourself
C. give your cousin a brochure on the juvenile detention center
D. offer your cousin a whip and a chair, similar to those used by the lion tamers
E. all of the above

If you chose *b,* you'll probably get into trouble, and the family will gossip about you. If you chose *a,* the same thing will happen. If you chose *c* or *d,* you'll probably never see any of them again (come to think of it, that could be the answer!).

But if you're like most of us, you'd like a peaceful and happy resolution to the chaos. Read on to see what our writers did when things got out of control—they survived, and so will you if you heed their advice.

Petty Complaints

Patty Swyden Sullivan

OUR ADULT CHILDREN LOVE their dogs and cats; and we love our children, but must we bond with their pets?

When our kids come to visit, the critters come. I will admit it straight out, I am not an enthusiastic animal lover. The love I do possess is best demonstrated from a distance; it is most definitely not put to the test when these four-legged, fur-shedding mammoths park their behinds on Great Aunt Lorraine's Oriental rug. Our home was not designed for free-range zones. But what are parents to do when their children cannot bear the thought of leaving their beloved dogs

(Hercules, Samson, and Hulk) in a kennel when they come to visit?

I acknowledge that dogs are often heroic and provide tremendous service to humans. They are invaluable to the disabled, and they are loyal companions for shut-ins. Does this concession mitigate my campaign for legislation limiting their activity to these categories? What, too restrictive? Okay, add police and security guards to their sanctioned designations—anything but *houseguest!*

Unfortunately, my children loudly disagree with me. We waste most of our time together arguing the merits of their traveling companions. My children are *indignant* (an attitude that should be reserved for maligned mothers and the wrongfully imprisoned) that I value material possessions over the sensitivities of their living, breathing, panting, drooling, barking dogs.

Perhaps I could handle these animals better if they were smaller. My children must believe the bigger the breed, the deeper the love. Enter the German shepherd, the mastiff, and the golden retriever—lovable, even noble, animals when romping in fenced yards, parks, and other wide-open spaces. But inside my home they are creatures of mass destruction.

They thrash around our house, swish their tails with reckless abandonment, and knock over smaller less-substantial items: heirloom china cups innocently poised on the coffee table, meandering toddlers incapable of thwarting the magnetic appeal of living fur and drool, and various other mid-sized valuables that topple in their wake. I will childproof a home gladly, but I am miffed at having to safeguard possessions from beasts that are best suited to pulling farm wagons. See? The opportunities are endless for these misappropriated giants.

Even asleep, these pony-sized intruders offer no respite. As they slumber, they snore, whine, and hack, all the while exuding foul blasts of dog breath. I won't go into detail about the rear ends of these creatures, but think of an intermittent wind reminiscent of the lingering stench from a sewage dump.

Another unavoidable annoyance is "their business." The three of them are steadfast, if not orderly, in their toilet habits. One dog barks to go out, another one barks to come in. This nonstop parade deposits volumes of refuse over my carpets—dirt, clumps of dead leaves and grass—and that's in dry weather. Wet weather is disastrous. I command the doorway with enough old rags to wax twenty Bentleys. Although my speed, dexterity, and form have earned me tremendous attention, paw-wiping is my least favorite event: It comes right behind hog-tying.

I would be remiss to omit the feline members of our children's clan; Schnook-ums and Ms. Jewels. But my list of grievances about them is shorter. They maintain a quieter decorum unless they are coughing up fur balls or expressing displeasure at being noticed. In our home, the visiting cats are sequestered to prevent war with the visiting dogs. The dogs sit outside the closed door whimpering, sniffing, and clawing at the carpet as they try to reach the kitties' booty. I confess to a perverted pleasure in watching the dogs in their pointless vigil. Then again, my pet problem could resolve itself if I cracked the door a smidge; after all, somebody ought to check on those little kitties . . . shouldn't they?

Before you call the humane society to report me, I promise to never hurt, tease, or neglect animals in my care. What I will promise is to pay for each of my grand-pets to enjoy personal attention in the privacy of their own homes by a reliable dog-and-cat sitter so that the next time my children come to visit we can do just that, instead of fighting like—you know what's coming—cats and dogs.

SURVIVAL HINTS

1. Offer to pay for the pet sitter or kennel.
2. Keep a doghouse handy for Fido's visits.
3. If possible, pay for a pet-friendly hotel for your guests and their furry friends.

As If Eight Weren't Enough

Mattie Hays

BACK IN THE OLD DAYS, families were huge in my clan. Each aunt and uncle produced—on average—five cousins.

In my family, keeping up with the rest of the family was always an issue. If they had it, we had to have it, too. They got a pool. We got a pool. They got a dog. We got a dog. They bought a second home. We bought a second home. You get the idea. Only everything we did had to be just one point better than whatever they did.

Everything, that is, except for having kids. My parents had three. My mother was sane. My Aunt Eve, on the other hand, broke the family average and produced seven (and one on the way).

Yes, I said, *seven.* Small ones, big ones, and ones that looked like monkeys, frogs, and toads. Some were loud, others were just part of the décor. We were a tight-knit family, and we used to spend every free moment at one house or another, bunched up together like an army of soldiers trying to keep warm on a cold winter's night.

On one particular day, dear Aunt Eve looked as if she had swallowed a small truck. She was huge, enormous, even. The poor woman had a hard time fitting her belly through the doorway, that's how gigantic she was.

She was ready to blow. Two weeks overdue for kid number eight, and mother of a three-ringed circus. As I look back, I really don't know how she did it.

It was about ninety-five degrees on this hot August day. Auntie Eve, sweating like an overweight construction worker paving a road in midtown Manhattan, decided to send the men out to get some ice cream for the kids. Or so she said. Now we all knew damn well she wanted the ice cream to cool off her gargantuan body, which was okay with us because we'd be the beneficiaries of her white lie and, frankly, she was starting to look sort of scary. She was flushed and getting redder by the minute.

Her three-ringed circus was running in and out of our pool, through the house, and back out the door, driving my sane, three-child mother off the deep end.

Suddenly Auntie Eve screamed out an *"Oh, no."* Along with that gushed a puddle of water at her feet. "My God, she's gonna blow," I thought. I ran for cover.

"It's time. She says get Tommy," my mother shouted.

Of course, Uncle Tommy had just been sent to the ice cream store, and my father had gone with him. Now I don't know about your family, but back then, in mine, none of the women drove cars. In fact, to this day, I don't think my Aunt Eve drives a car. Well, with all those kids, I am sure she doesn't have trouble getting around, kind of like Driving Miss Evey, the kids and grandkids playing chauffeur.

Unsure of what to do next without a driver, my mother reminded Aunt Eve that she had sent the men out and assured her that they would be back shortly. Mom called the doctor, and he said he was on his way. Yes, these were the good old days when doctors still made house calls.

To make my aunt more comfortable, Mom made her lie down on her bed. By now, not only were Aunt Eve's kids making a mess of the always tidy home, but here was a woman giving birth in my parent's bed.

I am sure that if my mother had to do this all over again, my aunt would be lying out in the grass; but for now the bed it was. You would think that after giving birth to seven kids the eighth would be pretty easy.

But Aunt Eve screamed and howled like a banshee. It was ear-piercing. Not to mention the disgusting mess. This baby was on its way, and it wasn't waiting for anyone or anything, ice cream included.

It wanted out.

And out it came, like a rocket on its way to the moon. It shot out and onto the bed. Luckily, my mother caught number eight before it hit the floor.

The doctor arrived just as Auntie Eve let out her last screech, and baby number nine came into the world.

"Twins!" Eve gasped, stunned.

"Twins," my mother said, even more shocked than Eve.

"Two," the doctor said. He was even more surprised than my mother.

Our happy family gathering had just grown a little bigger than we had expected!

SURVIVAL HINTS

1. Be thankful for the advancements of technology—if you're carrying twins, at least you'll know!
2. If it's larger than the opening it needs to go through, maybe it should take another route.
3. If you want ice cream, sometimes it's better to get it yourself.

Picky Eaters

Ginny Chandoha

AFTER WE'D MOVED TO our new house, my niece wanted to visit and bring her two young boys. My husband and I both have serious food allergies, so I am accustomed to asking prospective visitors what their special needs are and preparing meals accordingly. I was greatly relieved when my niece gave me convincing reassurance: "We'll eat anything, and the kids are easy."

But it didn't work out that way. From the moment of their arrival, every meal I prepared turned out to contain something that one or both boys didn't like and/or wouldn't eat. The youngest boy wanted chocolate milk, but it had to be extra chocolatey and heated to a specific temperature. He also wanted to drink it with a straw, but the straw couldn't be a plain, straight straw; no, it had to be one that had a ribbed end so that it would bend. He wouldn't eat anything green, and he wouldn't touch anything with mayonnaise in it. The eldest son was only slightly better, not liking spaghetti sauce or any type of pasta. He wouldn't touch fish, and he didn't like mashed potatoes, either. Neither of them liked eggs. "I thought you said they ate *everything,* that they were *easy!*" I hissed at my niece. But she just shrugged.

When I learned that they all liked steak, I marinated several for a day or two in a marinade that everyone else raves about. I served the steak, expecting them to enjoy the tasty meal, but apparently it couldn't quite measure up to the steaks my niece prepares. My joy in cooking quickly turned to disappointment.

With growing exasperation, I gave up trying to feed these kids and informed my niece that she and her boys could fend for themselves. I watched as she made hot dogs and grilled cheese sandwiches. "So what you meant when you said they eat anything is that they'll eat anything that's junk food!" I half joked.

On their last morning with us, my niece asked me to make the same waffles I'd made for her when she was a child. They were quickly gobbled up by all, and I wished I'd known the boys would love eating them from the get go. I made a mental note to stock up on hot dogs, hamburgers, sliced cheese, frozen pizza, and straws that bend in preparation for the next time they come to visit. And to make plenty of waffles!

As we waved goodbye to them, I turned to my husband and announced: "Look on the bright side. With all the leftovers, we won't have to cook anything for a long time!"

SURVIVAL HINTS

1. When cooking for children you don't know well, it's best to ask the parents *exactly* what the kids eat.
2. To get the real picture, try having the mom or dad describe what their kids have eaten in the last few days.
3. Try not to cook anything exotic, marinated, or covered in sauce.
4. Usually the plainer the better is the best policy when cooking for most children.
5. If you really can't get any advance information, go with simple dishes.
6. Be certain to include bread, pasta, and rice at every meal to be sure there's something the children will eat.
7. Remember, you can always add flavors, salt, spices, or herbs after the food is served, but it's hard to remove them once they're in the dish.

7

When They Help Too Much

It's always nice to have help, or at least people who are willing to help when you're entertaining. But sometimes helping hands, especially if there are too many of them, can become more of a real hindrance.

What do you do when too many cooks literally spoil the broth? Take the following quiz and see how you fare:

Sanity Quiz

You're having a family get-together. Your kitchen is the smallest room in the house. Naturally, not only does every invited guest decide to take up residence in there while you are trying to prepare the meal but they all want to help. You have too many hands in the pot and are literally tripping over yourself. With all the commotion, you won't even remember what you're preparing. How do you handle it without whacking someone with a skillet?

Do you

A. politely ask them all to leave the kitchen
B. sit down and let them finish up for you

C. grab the car keys and go out to eat without them
D. change your plans and order in
E. send them all home
F. Some or all of the above

As much as you may want to try *c* or *e,* they would be rude and inhospitable. And although *b* might be tempting, who knows what the dinner will turn into—you probably won't be able to eat it either! And *d* isn't practical—you're already midstream. So can you really try *a*? Not likely. Besides, you do love their company—they're just driving you nuts while you cook.

Some of our writers decided that the best course is to sit back and let them take over—this is great if you're pregnant, have a lot of small kids or pets or both, or need to go out of town on business. But if your intention is to spend time with your guests without being driven insane, you need to find a way to distract or amuse them so they will stay out of your hair.

Read on, and learn from the masters how to save your sanity, and have a few laughs along the way.

Sheer Heaven

Carol Kilgore

MY FIRST BABY WAS born two weeks early, a shock for all of us. I had one last project to complete at work before taking leave when . . . surprise! Four years later, when I became pregnant again, the doctor predicted the second birth would be early, too.

We lived half a continent away from our immediate families, and my aunt volunteered to come take charge of things while I was out of action. Because of the likelihood of the baby's early arrival, Auntie showed up three weeks before the due date, just to make sure.

I was excited to see her and also thrilled about the immediate help she would offer. This baby consumed every millimeter of space in my ever-expanding belly. With effort, I could lower myself to the floor of the bathroom to clean the tub. But the week before Auntie's arrival, I could no longer get close enough to it to clean the far side. Sitting on the ledge was worse.

Truth be told, I hated cleaning the darn tub. But I enjoyed the satisfaction of seeing our home clean and tidy even if I didn't always enjoy the tedious work of keeping it that way. Sometimes I could convince my four-year-old to help. That took longer, but it was more fun if we made housework into a game. I tried to get him to attach little Comet-doused sponges to his feet and clean the tub, but he ran away fast from that one.

The first week with Auntie was sheer heaven. She cleaned like a whirlwind compared to my duck-waddle pace. That tub sparkled, but my skies darkened. It should be fun watching someone else do my work. Why did I feel guilty?

Week two passed. Auntie was a dirt warrior: She attacked my fridge, oven, and kitchen cupboards. She was never accusatory, but once or twice I thought I spotted a disapproving glint in her eye. Through it all, I endured her patient teachings about the proper way to clean. Who knew that Auntie had a thing about dust bunnies? My motto was a little unseen dirt kept you healthy, but I forced a smile and I always thanked her for her advice and hard work. We would survive living the lifestyle of the super-clean for a few weeks.

Week three came and went. So did the due date. My doctor and my aunt thought I had miscalculated. I assured them I had not.

Everyone's nerves were on edge, especially mine. To top it off, the baby had become so large that only two pairs of my maternity pants still fit.

Near the beginning of the fourth week of Auntie's visit, as I stood well back from the sink to wash the breakfast dishes, Auntie said, "You look so uncomfortable. I'll start cooking and doing the dishes."

Uh-uh. No way—it wasn't happening. Some fast thinking was called for: "I like to cook, and it's relaxing."

"At least let me do the dishes."

"How about you do them at breakfast, and I'll clean up after lunch and dinner?"

We finally agreed on that. My family was spared Auntie's cooking. They didn't know she had a reputation, but I remembered the time she made homemade ice cream and forgot to put in the sugar.

Weeks four and five were insane. It seemed as though Auntie followed me around with a feather duster and a broom. Besides the cooking, about the only thing still under my control was the laundry. Our brightly colored clothes were safe from her hot-water-and-bleach fixation.

Week six the baby finally arrived, four weeks late, but a healthy nine pounds, fourteen ounces, complete with his daddy's long, skinny bird-like legs.

Our welcome-home dinner was one of Auntie's self-proclaimed Texas specialties—chicken and dumplings. I took a small, tentative bite. The food was delicious.

It was still good on the second night. But on the third night, the meal was broth with dumplings and bits of chicken. I said, "Tomorrow night, I'm making meatloaf."

Silence descended. I had caved in on many of the other skirmishes, but I knew it was important to pick the right battle to fight. This was it, and it was mine to win.

The next night, I made good on my statement. My fingers pushed through the ground beef and squeezed it with a satisfying *squish.* As the aromas of onion and garlic filled the kitchen, my mouth watered. That night, my meatloaf was the best ever.

Auntie stayed another week, just to make sure we could take care of ourselves. After we returned from seeing her off at the airport, I scrubbed the bathtub, luxuriating in those soothing, repetitive motions . . . and I welcomed the dust bunny that scooted out when I opened the door to the linen closet.

Sheer heaven.

SURVIVAL HINTS

1. Pick carefully the battles you want to fight.
2. Keep your sense of humor.
3. Be grateful that someone cares enough to help you out.

Mother 101

Pamela K. Brodowsky

WHAT IS IT ABOUT the mother–daughter relationship that always seems to make your life more complicated than it needs to be? Why do moms feel the direct need to put in their two-cents worth even when it hasn't been asked for? How does a mother who healed your every wound, hugged you when you were cold, kept you out of harm's way, and was always there for you suddenly turn into the person who now judges your every move?

Because she is a mom, that's how. That is what they are there to do.

When you think back, did you ask for that dating advice when you were sixteen? No, you just got it. Did you ask her what she thought of the man you planned to marry when you were twenty-one? No, she just told you. So what in the world makes you think she would stop when you moved out, got married, or had kids?

Grandkids just give our mothers a whole new wealth of information to toss our way. Oh, and you know that when moms ran out of reasons for their advice-giving, they resorted to the familiar "Because I said so."

Regardless of these judgmental ways, we still love our mothers dearly. After all, if it wasn't for them, we wouldn't be here.

My mom is usually a light-hearted soul. She usually tries to lend a helping hand and, believe me, it's appreciated. I have two kids, ten cats, and a *big* golden retriever. Oh, yeah, and a full-time job.

At times, you need to sacrifice attention to one to give it to another. The first "it can wait item" on my list of life is my house. If it's not a breathing thing, it can wait, that's my motto. But, you see, my motto drives my mother nuts. She cannot, and will not, stand for a messy house. Now notice that I say "messy," not "filthy." If it doesn't pass her white-gloved finger test, look out.

Mother comes to visit on Mondays, Wednesdays, and Fridays. That is, when she is in her light-hearted mood. Not only does she visit, but she cleans my house, folds the laundry, and does any dishes that happen to be left in the sink. I think it's a hell of a deal. Until she calls on Tuesday, Thursday, or Saturday, that is. On those days, I prefer not to answer the phone. And that is because those are her days for delivering her unwanted advice.

Now you must ask yourself this question: If something really bugged you, I mean down right under your skin bugged you, would you keep going back to its source? My commonsense answer to that would be "No." But then again, when you're a mom, sometimes your way of thinking has become altered. She doesn't see my messy house as an irritant to her, although it does irritate her, but as something she can fix and ultimately complain about.

I live here, it doesn't bother me. And, I will get to it in time, my time, not hers or anyone else's. If I had a dollar for every time Mom said "How can you stand living with all those animals?" I'd be rich.

Although my mother's desire for me to live in a spic-and-span house comes with its perks, the unwanted advice that follows is less than pleasing.

On one particular weekend, I had to leave town. My job requires me to travel from time to time, and I had an early Monday morning appointment in the city. My mother, the kind-hearted soul that she is, often stays at my house to watch my kids because my husband usually travels with me.

I was in a rush as usual, and I had a dinner appointment set for that evening; consequently, I left the house in a state of disarray. Kisses to everyone, out the door we went.

Arriving home the next day, I knew that some sort of surprise was in store. However, I had never bargained for what I was about to see. My mother, the compulsive spic-and-span woman, the lady who just can't stand the thought of my living with all those animals, had not only cleaned my house but also bathed each one of my animals!

I was greeted by ten wet cats, two clean kids, and a soaked golden retriever, all frolicking around my house. Everything smelled like clean, damp fur.

But when I turned the corner and saw my mother, shock set in. She had given my animals a thorough washing, but they, in turn, had soaked Mom from head to toe. Caught off guard by my early return, Mom had quickly tried to fluff her soaking wet, untidy hair, just as if she were totally relaxed and had been doing nothing more than eating bonbons and playing blocks with my children.

My immediate reaction, besides my loud laugh, was to run to my bedroom to grab the camera!

SURVIVAL HINTS

1. If your mom feels the need to come and clean your house, let her.
2. If she goes that extra step and tries to wash your pets, buy her a big bottle of pet shampoo.
3. Always have a camera loaded with film for those special Kodak moments.
4. Make sure you have plenty of towels when Mom baby-sits!

The Helpful Dinner Guest

Evelyn M. Fazio

I WAS FORTUNATE TO be blessed with truly wonderful parents. And my mother would do anything and everything to help anybody, anywhere, especially me.

This is great when you're in need of chicken soup or have to take a package to the post office but you can't leave home because a repairman is working on your house. As for my father, well, he could fix anything, and told the funniest stories you'd ever want to hear.

However, having my parents over for dinner used to be a challenge sometimes. It's not that they were picky eaters, or that they were complainers or fussy. No. In those ways, they were always perfect guests.

The problem was something else entirely. You see, Mom is just a little too "helpful" sometimes when you're trying to prepare dinner.

Mom used to drive me crazy whenever she came to dinner. Like a jack-in-the-box, she would pop out of her chair and zip right into the kitchen to "help." This would be fine if I lived in one of those McMansions equipped with a huge trophy kitchen. But I live in a one-bedroom condo, which is just fine for me, my cats, and my laptop.

My "helper" was always telling me the right way to do whatever it was: "Put the dish in this way, Honey," or, "I always cook the string beans a lot longer, Honey," or, "Can I do something to help you, Honey?"

In short, the perfect mother was driving me nuts!

Luckily, I came upon a solution. I found that the best thing to do is to keep her occupied—somewhere, anywhere, besides the kitchen.

It happened one day, after I'd escorted her back to the living room for the twenty-fifth time to keep my father company: I had a brainstorm. Here was a way to keep her occupied, entertained, and out of my hair so that I could actually finish preparing the meal before we all shriveled into husks from starvation!

I put on a movie—a really engrossing one—*The Godfather*.

Being Italian, that pretty much did the trick. Now I could barely tear them away from the television and lure them into the dining room when the food was waiting on the table. We all enjoyed dinner, we talked about the movie, and I put the film back on as soon as we had finished eating so that I could clean up and prepare dessert and coffee.

I was helper-free for the remainder of their visit. I'm told that this strategy is similar to parents using a DVD to baby-sit their kids.

That evening was a great success, my parents went home happy with their leftovers, and I had made it through without pulling a single hair out of my head.

SURVIVAL HINTS

1. Find something to distract guests who want to help you in the kitchen; ask them to make a salad, entertain the kids, or help with homework.
2. Put on a great sporting event or film to keep them occupied.
3. Show home movies in which they have a starring role.
4. Invite other guests who will engross the "helpers" in conversation and keep them occupied and out of the kitchen.

The Marauding Rearranger

Glennie Ross

WHAT IS IT ABOUT your parents that can send you completely over the edge? It must be that they know you so well, that they know exactly which buttons to push, when, and how often. Or maybe it's just that they still think you're a child who needs help. Sometimes, however, they really go overboard.

Recently, my father came to stay at my house. He's a well-meaning sort, and a nice man, but sometimes he goes too far. During his last visit, I had to go out of town overnight on business in the middle of his week with me.

He's kind of the Felix Unger neat-nut type, and he has specific ideas about where things should go and how they should be arranged once there. This is a wonderful trait if you need help with a mess, or if you want to organize your new home and you've asked for help. He also keeps a nice tidy home that is a pleasure to visit.

But there's a catch to all this, and here it is: He's a pain in the neck as a houseguest. Here's one example. While I was on that aforementioned trip, he decided that he didn't agree with the setup of my linen closet. Apparently, it just wasn't up to his standards, or else I wasn't careful enough with my linen-closet maintenance.

So what did he do? He changed it. Every last towel, sheet, pillowcase, and washcloth was now neatly folded and in place, but on different shelves than where I'd left them. I prefer keeping things arranged by type, such as all the sheets together, all the towels somewhere else, the blankets on the bottom shelf because they're big and heavy.

Unfortunately, Dad had other ideas. He thinks they should be arranged by color, so that when one is making up a bed, say, in the guest room, one can find all the matching components for that room and its bathroom. No doubt carrying a Martha Stewart gene, he prefers the bedroom and bathroom to be color-coordinated, and he proceeded to make them so.

Thus I returned to rearranged linens. And that was only the beginning. Dad had actually taken it upon himself to undo work I'd done, thinking that his way was better, including the placement of my newly installed kitchen shelves, which he thought would be more usable over the sink rather than on the empty wall between the two windows where I actually wanted them.

He also apparently objected to one of my time-saving strategies. I live in a three-story house, and often I place items that have to be taken upstairs on the staircase or landings before I've gotten around to taking them all the way up.

Mr. Helpful decided that none of these items should be on the stairs, let alone go upstairs, so he took every one of them back down to the first floor and stowed them all in the closet of the guest room he was using! Imagine my surprise when I couldn't find the toilet paper for the third-floor bathroom that I'd left on the second-floor landing after some last-minute shopping the night before I left. Imagine my further surprise when I used the third-floor bathroom and there was neither toilet paper nor facial tissues on hand to get the jobs done. I was livid.

Next came the refrigerator. Even though I'd just cleaned it, Dad had not only re-cleaned it but also put everything back in a different spot from where it had been the day before. The meat drawer became the veggie drawer. The veggie drawer became the canned soda drawer. The butter was not in the butter slot but on the top shelf, and the egg holder had moved from the top shelf to the bottom shelf. The first time I went to make breakfast after I returned from my trip, I stood agape in front of the open door. It was alien territory. It was like living in a development where all the houses looked alike and I'd slept in the wrong one!

And that was not the end of it. Dad's attentions had been lavished on the pantry, the hall coat closet, and even the medicine chest—he had left no object in its original place, and I spent an entire day trying to make sense out of it all.

Finally, when I couldn't find my car keys, I lost my temper. I called him up and demanded to know where he had put them. He responded as follows:

"I put them on a nice new key holder I hung next to the door to the attached garage so you'd never have to go looking for them again. They are now so close to the car that I'm surprised you didn't find them right away!"

Mind you, I've always kept my car keys in a silver tray on a little hall table just so that I'd always be able to find them, and that's exactly where I left them before my trip. Why he took it upon himself to move them without mentioning it will be one of the great unsolved mysteries of my life.

I told Dad that he was driving me crazy, that he shouldn't have moved everything around in my house, and that now I had to spend time putting everything back into its original place where I actually wanted it, rather than where *he* thought it should be. I told him that I worked long hours and didn't have time to go on a treasure hunt every time I couldn't find something, and that it would take days to put everything back once I had actually found it all. I told him that because I was paying the mortgage, the utilities, the taxes, and all the other expenses, I was entitled to arrange my own life and possessions. After this diatribe, I was so angry that I signed off in a huff without giving him the chance to explain or argue.

About a week later, he called me, rather sheepishly: "Your phone call last week really caught me off guard," he said. "But you must understand that I do only what I think is right, and what makes the most sense." He obviously still did not understand that these decisions are not up to him! I tried explaining it all over again, but probably to no avail.

Next time Dad comes to house-sit, I'm locking him in the basement!

SURVIVAL HINTS

1. If your neat-nick relative is coming to house-sit, be sure to tell him or her not to move anything.
2. If your neat-nick relative is staying for more than one day, be sure to assign a task that will keep your guest too busy even to think about taking on extra tasks.
3. If you can manage it, hire someone to house-sit.
4. Try not to leave a neat-nick alone too long! You know what happens when hands are idle!

8

When They Won't Go Home

Visits from friends and family are wonderful so long as your guests know when to leave: when you're tired and falling asleep at the table, when they've been there too long and have nothing left to say but still won't budge, or when you've simply given up and gone to bed! What should you do?

Take our final test and measure your skills at coping with the ossified, immovable object known as the guest who won't go home:

Sanity Quiz

Your friend Julian has come to visit and has been with you since 8:00 a.m. It's now 10:00 p.m. and you are exhausted. You have to go to work in the morning and can barely keep your eyes open. Julian doesn't notice, or maybe he just doesn't care. Oblivion is beckoning, along with your bed.

Do you

A. tell Julian goodbye and stand up

B. just go to bed and leave him sitting on your sofa
C. throw him out
D. any of the above

We are all probably familiar with this situation, but what can you do, a friend is a friend, isn't he? But sometimes you have to resort to drastic measures.

Our writers came up with creative solutions and practical advice. No matter what, you'll come away with new ways to cope with those never-leaving guests.

Obviously, we've saved the best for last!

Homeland Security Memo

Kenneth P. Hastie

MARKED: Classified and Insensitive

TO: Those having a need to know how to: (A) get rid of houseguests earlier; (B) prevent them from staying in your domain in the future; or (C) just maintain control in an often uncontrollable situation.

FR: Those who know and who have shared your pain.

RE: *Special Houseguest Ops, Tactics and Strategies* (SHOTS). Caution: Use these more extreme methods only if you require desperate measures to move on to the "next plateau" of the "Houseguest Arts," that is, making them feel they've had a good visit with you without having them fully invade and threaten "your space."

Sure, you love 'em. You have no choice, it seems. But then, you also had little choice in having them as relatives in the first place, if they happen to be family. You just have them. That's all. You're stuck with them, like it or not. Our job here is to make tolerating them in larger time and proximity doses, on your turf, more acceptable.

If they happen to be your friends, and you're contemplating these tactics, well . . . shame on you. You should have picked better friends.

Either way, these are powerful, proven tactics and techniques that should be used only when you've absolutely had enough and need to solve the situation now—and in the future.

What follows is a short list of quick hard-hitting, get-them-out ideas that are both proven and also designed to get you thinking about additions to the list that fit your circumstances even better. (We're sure you can come up with plenty of ideas on your own!)

Remember, our goal is to get them out if they're in—and to get them to stay, the next time, in a nearby hotel instead of your cherished home and hearth. (More about that later in this document.) Anyway, here are some ideas to get you started.

- Absolutely make sure the only comfortable bed in the house is yours. Go out of your way to find your guests the most uncomfortable couch, hide-a-bed, or inflatable mattress possible. Futons may fit the bill here. The next morning, be sure to ask, "Did you sleep well?"
- If your guests are "morning people," sleep in as long as you possibly can. If they are late risers, be up early and crow like a rooster, explaining that you've always been an admirer of nature's early-morning wonders.
- Don't make the temperature too comfortable anywhere in the house where your guests congregate. Create drafty areas in winter. Dead air spots in summer. You get the idea.
- If you don't already own a cat, borrow or rent one. Many people are allergic to cats. Statistically, the percentages are in your favor. An allergic reaction can sometimes require prompt medical attention . . . often outside your home! At minimum, you'll likely make guests uncomfortable enough that they'll crave home—theirs!
- Absolutely don't serve better food than they can get at home. Sure they'll think you're a lousy cook, but they won't come back for seconds—and they may not even want to stay for dessert.

- Tell them about the squirrels in the attic—that you believe are not rabid—and that, knock on wood, they haven't fallen through the ceiling yet.
- To spice up your guests' stay, spontaneously argue loudly and often with your spouse or significant other. The look of discomfort on your guests' faces alone will be worth the play-acting you might have to fake (or not).
- Between battles, be as nauseatingly adoring of your spouse or significant other as possible. This tactic will make most people so uncomfortable that they will wish they had never left their hometown.
- If it can be prearranged, consider having furniture delivered during your "entertaining" and ask the guests to help move the existing furniture around to accommodate the new furniture. Hey, at least you'll have more hands to make lighter work! One caution, though: Make sure that no one from your newfound "work crew" has a bad back, or the potential for one. One accident with this sophisticated tactic and you may have company for even longer. Counterproductive.
- Whenever and wherever possible, discuss volatile topics such as politics, religion, and gun control. Try to take positions that you

already know will annoy your guests—whether or not you actually believe them. Often, the more outrageous you are, the better the strategy will work. They may think you're completely nuts and decide that it is actually not safe to be in the same house with you (much less *your* house)!

- Spend inordinate amounts of time in your bathroom(s). Essentially, cut off access whenever possible. Most people have something of a schedule in this regard, and if you can disrupt it, your lucky guests will be secretly screaming to go home—or, at minimum, they will ask you where the nearest gas station is so they can get "gassed up" for their travels. Very effective. For an added touch, you can repeatedly remind everyone about the sewage back-up last year that caused such heartache.
- For entertainment purposes, there is nothing better for bonding than sitting down collectively to watch a DVD. Make sure you put on something that you know your guests couldn't possibly like. If you prefer to take the more genteel route with this technique, by all means rent a movie that they might actually want to see. Just make sure they have to sit through some exhaustive

"preliminaries" (i.e., your wedding video, the graphic birthing of your children, your trip to the Poconos, etc.). Cold, stale popcorn helps, too.

- It's important to talk about your health maladies at length. People just love to hear about them. By all means, be repetitive and graphic wherever possible. Operations, scar-sharing are both good—and if you have anything that could remotely be considered communicable, be sure to highlight that, as well. It's the right thing to do.
- Rude body noises can sometimes be okay, contrary to popular belief—and particularly considering our goals here. Feel free. Live free. It's your home. Be you. Be all the wonder that *is* you. It's natural, after all. And wouldn't our friends and family want us to be ourselves? Of course. Let it rip!

Well, by now, you're probably getting the idea—and you can no doubt add to this basic list. There are indeed more extreme measures for certain goals.

Carry on, soldier. Your own homeland security is depending on you.

The Last Straw

Leah Jones

NOW I AM NOT one to be nasty, really I'm not. That is, unless you piss me off.

When my husband and I married, we rented this cute little log cabin pretty much out in the middle of nowhere. And by nowhere, I mean at least a thirty-minute drive on the long and winding pot-holed backwoods road to Podunk.

The town consisted of a barn and a firehouse. Oh, yeah, there was a post office—but I think that might have been inside the barn; at least, that would explain the odor the mail always brought with it.

We went out of our way to find this type of seclusion for good reason. We figured that by being so far away from friends and family we would cut down on visitors and we would have time to begin our new life together without extra interference. How wrong we were.

Moving away from them doesn't keep them away. It just lengthens their stay. My brother Mike, a thirty-something single at the time, still living at home with Mama, found that my house was a good escape.

At first, his visits were scattered and bearable. A dinner here, a dinner there, just stopping by on his way somewhere else (thirty miles out of the way), and this was all good and well.

My rule has always been that if it lasts for less than two hours, it's a good visit. If you can't say everything you have to say in two hours, maybe you should see an editor or a speech therapist.

Anyhow, Mike's visits became more frequent. Eventually, they were a daily ritual. It wasn't just dinner anymore. It was an invasion.

Mike would eat dinner, then lie around on the couch and stare at the boob tube (and I use that term on more than one level) for hours on end and in complete silence. I think he was silent because he was there *all* the time and didn't have anything left to say! Mike became part of the furniture, but he required more maintenance. My husband was losing it. "Get rid of him!" he'd hiss.

The situation got worse before it got better. The daily visits were now turning into overnight stays. I can still hear those horrible words: "Can I just crash here? I don't feel like driving *all* the way back home."

My first thoughts were, "You seem to have no trouble driving here, so you should have no trouble finding your way home." But at that point, I was still a softy, letting it slide, hoping that if I ignored it long enough, my brother would just go away. But in my heart, I knew I had a problem.

But then, on his next visit, he was toting a bag—a bag of clothes, that is. Now not only was he wearing out his welcome, he was planning ahead for the length of his stay. He was moving in, slowly and sneakily.

That was the day I lost it. I had had my fill. Mike was being an inconsiderate jerk by assuming he could just plant himself in my house to escape his uncomfortable living situation. My husband was furious because we hadn't been alone in our own house for well over a month, and I was sick and tired of having to clean up after, feed, and listen to an uninvited and unwanted guest. So I took matters into my own hands.

Our television was on its way out. It was an old Magnavox that I had owned for years before I got married, and I had no problem compromising its well-being to save my sanity.

While Mike sat perched on my front porch, sloshing down the remainder of his daily beer allotment, I went off to the basement. Rooting through my husband's tool box, I snatched up the wire cutters and went up the two floors of the cabin to the living-room loft. There she sat—my fifteen-year-old idiot box. Yanking the electrical cord from the outlet, I chopped off the end in one quick snap. Without even a backward glance, down the stairs I went.

That night after dinner, I announced, "The TV is dead." I don't know how he knew, or even whether he did at that moment, but my husband looked at me with a grin of sheer delight. Mike's only reply was "What?" I repeated, "The TV is dead."

"Oh, man, I gotta get going." That night he packed up his bag and went on his way, back to his own home.

You see, after all the inconvenience he had caused us, making him a little less comfortable proved invaluable.

After assuring ourselves that Mike was far enough on his way down the long and winding road that we wouldn't be tailing him, my husband and I were off to the television store. Alone at last!

SURVIVAL HINTS

1. If you want to get rid of the boob, get rid of the tube.

2. It's always beneficial to give back a bit of what you are being handed.
3. Problems just don't go away; they need to be addressed.
4. Make sure that if you move to escape family and friends, you live farther away than a thirty-minute drive.

No Sense of Departure

Omega Downs

HEY, LOOK, WE ALL have friends. Some of us have more than others, but we all have at least one. Some are fun, some are annoying, some are downright funny, and some are a giant pain in the . . . well, we won't go there.

My husband's buddies fall into the we won't go there category. Not because they are bad people, truly they are not. They just never know when the hell to beat the bricks, hit the road, or, more simply, get their own damn lives.

One in particular quickly comes to mind. I can't say why—oh, wait a minute, yes, I can. It's because he's sitting across the room from me right now, where I imagine he will still be in the wee hours of the morning.

Let me introduce you to Steve. I would say Steve is my husband's next-to-best friend, the brother of the best friend, but runner-up when it comes to titles. Steve doesn't visit often, maybe only two to three times a month, which I find to be the perfect number of visits, or maybe a bit excessive. However, the frequency is not the problem with this situation. The duration, on the other hand, is.

You see, Steve is middle-aged and single, and he does not have many options for a social life. Although he is outgoing, he truly does not know when it's time to *go.* Now don't get me wrong. I like Steve. I think he is funny, intelligent, and, for the most part, a good addition to our lives. I normally think those thoughts from daybreak till about 10:00 p.m., at which point my feelings change.

You see, Steve likes to talk. And I don't just mean casual updates about what's happened in his life since his last visit. I mean the whole recap from birth onwards. His stories encompass every minor detail and grow into long, drawn-out sagas, complete with sound effects. It's not so much the stories that bother me because I have heard them all. I don't even have to pay attention anymore; I can daydream and just pickup on a key word and chime in if a response is expected. No, the problem is the length, duration, and repetitiveness of the stories. I really don't know how my husband stands it—he was a participant in most of the stories, so not only is he familiar with the details, he also lived them.

On one particular visit, I was very tired. My two young children had given me a run for my money that day and all I wanted to do was go to sleep. My husband and Steve had been out fishing all day and had just made it back in time for supper. Lucky me!

The dinner thing was done. Throughout the meal, I had listened to Steve telling me just how tired he was from fishing on some quiet pristine lake all day. I fed him coffee and dessert, and now it was time for him to go. But he wasn't going. He was staying. I knew that my husband was aware of the romper-room day I'd had. And his day in a boat with motor-mouth had left him looking a bit frayed himself.

Being in tune with my exhaustion, my husband tried to take the initiative. "I really gotta get some sleep," he said. Well, that flew right over Steve's head, like a kite on a windy day at the beach. Steve just took my husband's comment as a lead-in to another monologue about how tired *he* was.

"Would you just get the hell out?" I was thinking. But I couldn't say it. That would be rude. My being rude on top of his ignorance could make things ugly.

It was now cresting 10:30, and we were all still perched around the most uncomfortable kitchen table ever made. Then Steve's cell phone rang. I began to pray. God, please let it be an emergency. Please let it be a call for help. Please let it be the president of the United States calling for Steve's thorough insight; please let it be anything to get this slug out of my damn kitchen so that I can go the hell to sleep.

But it wasn't any of the above. It was just a girl he dates who wanted to chat. Rather than finishing up with us and going home to call her back, Steve sat at my kitchen table for twenty minutes talking on his phone. But this time he wasn't even talking. He was just listening. Steve could not get a word in edgewise with this girl. We could clearly hear her as we sat across the table; I don't think she stopped even once to take in a breath of air. Could there really be someone out there worse than Steve?

My patience was wearing thin at this point, and my husband was noticing. As Steve raised his hand to make the little "quack, quack" gesture to indicate that his girlfriend "talks too much," I almost fell off my chair in utter disbelief. If this wasn't the pot calling the kettle black, I don't know what is. The phone conversation finally came to an end, and Steve said, "Oh man, she never shuts up." Well, that is when I finally shot my rockets into orbit. Not only was he criticizing someone else for doing the same thing he does constantly but now he was implying that talking too much is a so-called woman thing.

"Oh, Steve," I thought, "you are treading on the territory of the unknown. For your sake and general well-being, I suggest a discreet tail-between-your-legs retreat. A quick get-up-and-go."

At first, I tried to be tactful. I stood up and pushed in my chair, thinking that the use of body language would do it for him, or should I say for me. But Steve showed no reaction. So I sat back down. I tried it again. I yawned a loud "I'm tired and getting annoyed" yawn that clearly couldn't be missed, and again stood up, this time shoving my chair in with a bit of force. Nothing!

He just went on and on about how much women talk. That did it for me. My husband could no longer save Steve. It was time for him to go. But still I gave him once last chance to be on his way. Again, he remained blissfully ignorant of our aggravation.

I began at the far end of the house. Room by room I went, shutting off the lights and closing the doors. When I had darkened every room but the kitchen, the only remaining light was the one above the kitchen table. My husband by now was cringing, wondering what I was going to do next. With a delighted grin I said, "Let's call it a night." Before Steve could grunt or acknowledge that I had said anything, I snapped off the kitchen light and left the men sitting in darkness.

And, for the very first time in his life, I think Steve was both speechless *and* saw the light, or the lack of it!

SURVIVAL HINTS

1. Sometimes body language works better than plain English.
2. To spare feelings, show what's on your mind instead of saying it.
3. It's your house, throw them out.
4. If all else fails, just switch off the lights and go to bed.

Acknowledgments

We would like to acknowledge our wonderful editor, Marnie Cochran, executive editor at Da Capo Press, for instantly getting it when we first called to talk about our idea for the Staying Sane series. From the beginning, Marnie understood what we were trying to do, and has helped us immeasurably in making our vision for the series take shape. Even though we have probably driven her a little crazy sometimes, we hope that she'll stay sane through it all and for a long time to come. Thank you, Marnie, for everything we know you do for us, along with all the things we never even hear about. We both know how fortunate we are to have our series in your capable hands.

Next, we would like to thank the other members of the Da Capo Press staff for their efforts, input, and help, beginning with Alexis Rizzuto (assistant editor),

John Radziewicz (publisher), Liz Tzetzo (director of sales), and Erica Lawrence (production editor).

Finally, and most important, we send many thanks to our contributors, especially Ed Fitzgerald, Ken Hastie, Walt Heskes, Scoop Skalpien, Jimmy Jacobs, John Tomaino, Ginny Chandoha, Susan Berlin, and all the rest. Without you, this book and the many others would not exist. You are, indeed, some of the funniest people on Earth, and wonderful writers, too. Whether you are friends, clients, family, or people we just met, thanks for being part of the team!

Evelyn would like to acknowledge the help and encouragement of some family members and several "almost family members" who were invaluable in keeping her sane for a very long time: my mother, who ran errands, brought in food, and otherwise helped me when I was chained to my laptop working on this series; Win Huppuch, my mentor and dear friend, who taught me everything I know about publishing and a lot about life; Ellen Sander, who really is family after thirty-four years; Jude Cataldo, my sister by choice, and confidant of twenty-four years, who sometimes single-handedly has kept me sane; P. J. Dempsey, my colleague and friend of almost two decades, who connected me with Pam and contributed a story (see what you got yourself into!); my neighbors and adopted family, the Seidmans, who regularly fed and entertained me on days when I otherwise would not have stopped working; and, Tony Sommo, who knows all my stories, even the ones I've forgotten. He has kept me laughing since 1976, and is probably one of the main reasons I'm still at least partially sane today.